To Ceylon Blackwell
'65

Best Wishes

Homer Cadrey

LEADERSHIP FITNESS

LEADERSHIP FITNESS

DEVELOPING AND REINFORCING
SUCCESSFUL, POSITIVE LEADERS

HOMER RICE

LONGSTREET PRESS
Athens, Georgia

LONGSTREET
PRESS

Published by
LONGSTREET PRESS, INC.
325 Milledge Avenue
Athens, Georgia 30601
www.longstreetpress.net

1st printing, 2004
ISBN: 1-56352-736-7

Printed in the United States of America

Jacket and book design by Burtch Hunter Design LLC

MY PERSONAL LIFE BLUEPRINT

NAME   _____

DATE   _____

Once you sign your name and date, this manuscript becomes YOUR guide to become a positve, successful leader. Utilize the information to fit your needs and style. May you become "fit" to the be the Ultimate Leader in Charge!

FOREWORD

Paul Meyer
Founder-Chairman of the Board
Success Motivation® International, Inc.

Even as a youngster, Homer Rice was gathering information that would help him write *Leadership Fitness: Developing and Reinforcing Successful, Positive Leaders.* As a twelve-year-old, Homer read a compelling book on goal-setting his father gave him for his birthday. This book challenged its readers to consider how to approach life and to search for the secrets of success. Homer took the mandate seriously and began a life-long habit of writing down goals for every area of his life. And thus began the rich life experiences that make Homer Rice uniquely qualified to write this outstanding book.

Achieving goals early in his life convinced Homer of the power of goal setting. These early successes also made him aware of the wellspring of wisdom in good books. He continued his search for the keys to success by reading the best books ever written on the topic. Homer's quest for knowledge resulted in his becoming an even more fervent advocate of committing one's goals to writing.

In addition, Homer identified from his comprehensive reading the significant elements of success: attitude, desire, belief, visualization, spaced repetition, habits, and focus. Homer's studies also led him to believe that true and lasting success comes only to those who set and achieve goals in all areas of life.

Investing life in studying, teaching, and practicing success principles created the opportunity for Homer and me to meet decades ago. I had been on an intense journey quite similar to

Homer's in search of the keys to a life of positive achievement. Like Homer, I had a burning desire to share this phenomenal "secret" with others. In 1960 I founded my flagship company and dedicated it to "motivating people to their full potential." I began writing and marketing information on how to set goals in every area of life and how to reach them by marshaling the powerful forces of a positive attitude, desire, belief, visualization, and all the other elements of success Homer and I had identified independently in our own journeys.

Our mutual zeal and commitment to learning more about success and sharing this information with others created an instantaneous bond. We enjoyed doing some writing together and kept up with each other over the years. Homer earned phenomenal success described more specifically elsewhere in this book. I also earned personal and financial success as my company and its affiliated companies spread throughout the United States and to more than sixty countries speaking twenty-three languages.

I believe my business background qualifies me as a credible judge of this book. While I treasure my friendship with Homer, that relationship is not the sole reason I recommend his book. I encourage you to read it because it is based on valid principles that have worked for me for more than five decades.

In a book full of invaluable truths, my favorite is, *In order to lead others, you must first become the person you want to be.* Homer never challenged anyone to be anything he was not willing to work toward becoming himself. I admire him for taking this stand, along with many others he has taken in his life. Homer, for example, never rested on his laurels. Although decades ago he reached countless pinnacles of success, he kept setting new worthwhile goals – and reaching them. What is even more gratifying is how his goals always seemed to be driven by the best interest of others. Homer Rice is a true leader.

The language of *Leadership Fitness* is straightforward and

reader friendly. The anecdotes and examples are interesting, and they add validity and credibility to the message. Embedded within these compelling pages is nothing short of a full-blown Ph.D. course of study. Homer Rice has distilled into one great book the important success and leadership principles of the ages. This book is a culmination of Homer's extraordinary life and career. I congratulate him for writing it, and I commend you for reading it. When you put into action the powerful content of Homer Rice's book, your life will never be the same.

Someone once said that success is not measured only by your climbing the ladder to success but by the number of people you helped climb that ladder. If this is true, and I believe it is, then Homer Rice is certainly one of the most successful leaders I have been privileged to know or even know about.

Read *Leadership Fitness: Developing and Reinforcing Successful, Positive Leaders* and join the legions of others whom Homer Rice has led to success beyond their wildest dreams. You will be astonished at what you can do.

PAUL J. MEYER

Founder of Success Motivation® International, Inc.
and 40-plus other companies
New York Times Best-Selling Author
Latest book: *Unlocking Your Legacy: 25 Keys for Success*
www.pauljmeyer.com

ACKNOWLEDGEMENTS

After authoring *Lessons for Leaders* (Longstreet Press) in 2000, I received letter after letter from people seeking more information on The Attitude Technique Philosophy, a Total Person-Total Success concept. No doubt, this stimulated me to think in terms of another book. I made the decision to include another manuscript on positive leadership development in my next five-year plan of goals. My "commitment" began the task. As I explain in this book, accomplishing a goal begins with "I", but actually making it happen requires others, which means the goal ends in "we." The team does it!

I needed a complete "squad" to work through and complete *Leadership Fitness*. The key was a disciplined approach: writing every day. It may have been ten minutes or several hours, but I did something each day. Once a lesson was completed, my long-time administrative assistant, Ann Harrell, typed the notes into a clean copy. As with *Lessons for Leaders*, I then turned to Elizabeth Haven Hawley, an astute doctoral student and American history instructor at Georgia Tech. While working on her own dissertation, Haven used her experience as a former journalism major and typesetter to edit my writing, helping to bring the manuscript from rough copy into a cohesive form. She again worked miracles, and the book took shape with positive results. Chuck Perry later edited the final version to make it book-ready.

Input from many people helped influence the final shape of the message of *Leadership Fitness*, and they are listed in Appendix "I" and on pages 160-165 of the Afterword (the latter focusing on the Leadership Fitness class of 2003). Corrections, additions, interviews, articles, and research by all of these people made this book happen. I thank them for their sincere efforts. As with the last book, I asked Bob Harty, executive director of Georgia Tech's

Institute Communications and Public Affairs department and an expert on publications, to critique the final copy. When Bob gave his blessings, I knew we had passed the test.

Before the completed copy was ready for the publisher, Ann Harrell became ill and passed away on October 4, 2003. What a wonderful human being she was – loved by everyone who knew her and a pillar of strength in the Georgia Tech Athletic Association. Surely she is in heaven smiling down on us as we struggle on without her tender, loving care. She will be sorely missed but, knowing Ann as I do, she would be disappointed if we did not carry on to do our very best. She was *always* at her best.

The final stage: Is the book worthy of publication and distribution? I sent a pre-press copy to the top people in various fields for their assessments. I asked Paul J. Meyer, founder of Success Motivation® International and a *New York Times* best-selling author, to review the material and, if so inclined, to consider writing the Foreword to the book. Paul is a pioneer of the motivation and leadership industry. His program materials have sold more than $2 billion worldwide – more than any other author in this field. Paul is a true "giver" (read *The Joy and Responsibility of Stewardship*) and a dear friend for more than forty years. He taught me the principle of the Total Person that shaped my life and gave me the idea to begin and implement a similar program for student-athletes throughout the colleges and universities in America and foreign lands. I certainly owe him much for his influence upon my work through the years. I knew Paul would be totally honest in his evaluation of *Leadership Fitness*. I was excited and extremely happy when he gave his approval and agreed to contribute the Foreword.

From the business world, I gained assistance from J. C. "Bud" Shaw, founder and past chairman of the board of Shaw Industries, the world's largest carpet industry. Bud is the ultimate leader in the business world, yet he has made time in his schedule through the years to visit my Leadership Fitness Class and to offer his positive advice to the students at Georgia Tech. During my years as director of athletics, he always supported programs benefiting student-athletes. His involvement usually assured the success of any program.

In writing *Leadership Fitness*, multiple memories popped from my human computer for suggestions and thoughts. One day I thought of Danny Lotz, a good friend and former outstanding athlete at the University of North Carolina. Danny became a prominent dentist in Raleigh, NC, after graduation. When I was director of athletics at UNC, I invited Danny to a football game and to sit in my box. He came accompanied by his wife Anne and her distinguished parents, Dr. and Mrs. Billy Graham. My wife's mother was visiting us at the time, and we were all ecstatic that this great spiritual leader would be seated in our box. Billy asked me to play a part in his crusade, which was taking place in nearby Raleigh the following week. I was honored by his request. Afterward, whenever my wife Phyllis and I attended the Fellowship of Christian Athletes conference each summer in Black Mountain, NC, we were always invited to visit the Grahams' home nearby. As time went on, their daughter Anne also became a prominent spiritual leader. Her books, lectures, TV and radio appearances brought belief in God to millions around the world through her "Angel Ministries" programs. I am convinced that successful, positive leaders must incorporate a spiritual aspect into their lives. Belief in God is a foundation of Leadership Fitness. I wondered if Dr. Danny Lotz would read *Leadership Fitness* and endorse its contents. A quick call to Danny confirmed that he would.

It finally was time to seek out those in the professional world who knew of my work over the years as a coach, teacher, administrator, and person. This would be the true test of the validity of *Leadership Fitness*.

From the coaching profession, who could be better than

Grant Teaff, executive director of the American Football Coaching Association? Grant was National Coach of the Year while coaching at Baylor University, where he had phenomenal success and currently provides tremendous positive leadership for football coaches at all levels. Grant provided the Foreword for *Lessons for Leaders*. Next I turned to athletic administration, calling Mike Cleary, long-time executive director of the National Association of the Collegiate Directors of Athletics. NACDA represents all colleges and universities on every level throughout the country and worldwide, and Mike's leadership has steered this organization to the top of the ladder. From the NCAA Divison-1 Athletic Directors came Executive Director Dutch Baughman, representing the top 117 universities in the United States. Dutch has provided the positive leadership to make good things happen for all of athletic administration. He has promoted the CHAMPS program that encourages the right ethics for intercollegiate athletics.

Colleagues such as Gene Corrigan – former director of athletics at the University of Virginia and at Notre Dame, commissioner of the Atlantic Coast Conference, and president of the National Collegiate Athletic Association – have also endorsed the book. My first collegiate administrative post was as director of athletics at the University of North Carolina, and the first visitor to my office was Gene Corrigan. We became instant friends and worked together for the betterment of student-athletes from that point forward. Gene is a super positive leader.

When I think of the giants in the field of preventive medicine, there is no one higher than Dr. Kenneth H. Cooper. This man may have saved many lives by developing the aerobic program for good health. No leader can be fit for the role without living a lifestyle that promotes good health. I have made many trips to Dr. Cooper's Aerobic Center in Dallas, TX. It's always a privilege to visit with Ken and get the latest news in good preventive health. His books are a must-read for aspiring leaders.

As I've noted in Appendix I on pages 217-219 and throughout these pages, this book was put together with aid from many people. It is an accumulation of notes, interviews, research, wisdom from speakers to classes, past writings, memories, and other people's recollections of the facts. This book reflects many of my own strong feelings, all backed by personal experience in finding the best approach to becoming a successful, positive leader. The good results have been overwhelming. To the best of my knowledge, all the data is accurate – and even my elaborations are based on true stories! I began jotting down notes for future use after my twelfth birthday, and later I decided to record my involvement in my profession. This book is my seventh to be published.

Successful seasons on the gridiron brought requests to speak at national clinics and to write articles for sports magazines, along with authors asking me to contribute to their books. Then one day a letter came from Prentice-Hall Publishing Co. to author a book for the Coaches' Book Club. That brought forth the *Explosive Short-T / Homer Rice on Triple Option Football*, and *The Air Option* (co-authored with Steve Moore).

When my football coaching ended and athletic administration began, I turned to writing books about leadership, such as *Leadership in Athletics* (Paul Meyer's Success Motivation® International, Inc.), *Leadership for Leaders* (MacGregor Sports), and *Lessons for Leaders* (Longstreet Press).

Leadership Fitness is the base for successful positive leadership. Whatever field you are engaged in or about to enter will require study and skills development in order to accomplish your goals in that area. But it is imperative to get your life into shape first. This program offers the ingredients to begin that project.

PREFACE

Scientists tell us that billions of years ago a "Big Bang" occurred. Theologians affirm that a Supreme Being – God – brought this about, resulting in the cosmos: earth, moon, sun, solar system, galaxies, and an endless expanse of planets throughout the universe. The *piece de resistance* of this creative process is human beings, creatures with brains and the power to think, to choose, to control and to create. We have minds of our own, minds that function both consciously and subconsciously.

This mental activity operates incessantly, serving as the most sophisticated computer every built. Our inner computer can be programmed for negative or positive responses, and designed to build or to destroy. It is precisely this cognitive capability that makes us human: to think abstractly; to reflect on ourselves; to govern our behavior; to make value judgments; to set goals; to organize; and to establish relationships – all for good or ill.

Leadership is the key to personal and social well-being. That is what this book is about: developing positive leadership that contributes to the common good. Robert Frost said we do not so much believe in the future as we believe the future in. The future largely becomes what the world's people believe and practice. *Leadership Fitness* is a study in human fulfillment and a wholesome society. Each of us is either part of the solution or part of the problem. My hope in these pages is to encourage and enable positive, effective leaders.

HOMER RICE

DEDICATION

Each book I have authored has been dedicated to my family. First, to my dear wife, Phyllis. We met in the seventh grade in 1939. I asked her for a date, my first date, and she accepted. We took in a Saturday afternoon movie. She claims she had to pay her own way, and I have been paying for that mistake ever since! Soon I secretly declared that she would become my wife. After high school, World War II, and college, we were married in 1950. We have been fortunate to have three lovely and talented daughters: Nancy Hetherington, Phyllis Ingle, and Angela Miller. They in turn have given us seven wonderful grandchildren: Ryce Hetherington, Leigh Hetherington, Drew Hetherington, Jamie Ingle, Brian Ingle, David Miller, and Andrew Miller. I dedicate *Leadership Fitness* to our wonderful and very close family.

There are others that I must recognize, including my parents, Dr. Samuel and Grace Rice, whose memories continue to inspire me; my older brother Robert Cecil Rice, whom I tagged after as a youngster; and my high school coach, Ewell "Judge" Waddell. Coach Waddell had a profound influence upon my career choice. Having him hire me as his replacment at Highlands High School in Fort Thomas, KY, was, at the time, my ultimate achievement. Many others had a tremendous influence upon my career and life, but to mention all of them would be a book in itself. I have been most fortunate to have received so much from so many.

CONTENTS

LEADERSHIP
FITNESS

INTRODUCTION

As a student, athlete, teacher, coach, and athletic adminis-
trator, I have learned it takes a leader
to shape a team into a successful unit.
This process starts with "I"
and transforms into "we."
The Team does it!

In May 1997, I ended a forty-seven-year career in athletics by announcing my retirement as director of athletics and executive assistant to the president at Georgia Tech. Little did I know that another career was about to begin for me at the age of seventy. Georgia Tech President Wayne Clough invited me to consider serving as a development consultant for both the university and the Department of Athletics. That was not all. Dr. Gary Schuster, Dean of the College of Sciences, encouraged me to consider teaching. I accepted both invitations, and overnight I became an adjunct professor. I asked Dean Schuster the meaning of "adjunct," and he promptly replied that it meant **no pay**. The course would be one dear to my heart, however: It would explain the Attitude Technique philosophy, a total person, total success concept for leadership. The title for the course became "Leadership Fitness."

My book *Lessons for Leaders* was at that time being pub-lished by Longstreet Press. The book sold out in the first year.

Readers, along with publisher Scott Bard, encouraged me to follow up with a book that delved more deeply into my philosophy of positive leadership.

My class, comprised mostly of seniors, became the laboratory for research and development of that next book, *Leadership Fitness*. Those bright, energetic young men and women were the challengers who kept me on my toes while together we explored this extremely important subject. That class energized me not only to continue teaching but also to seek other ways of promoting effective leadership and positive life skills. They told me that they would probably forget many of their class assignments from Georgia Tech, but "Leadership Fitness" would give them something to carry with them for the rest of their lives. That message made me realize the importance of my involvement in educating leaders. I learned that the great effort I'd taken to develop a high-level version of the program was appreciated. The positive feedback has been overwhelming.

One feature that I added to class meetings was exposing students to individuals who were highly successful in many fields. These people visited and spoke to students on their respective subjects of expertise. Several of the people whom students found most engaging have been asked to contribute to this book.

During my years at Georgia Tech, the Athletic Association began a program for student-athletes that became known as the Student-Athlete Total Person Program. Started in 1980, the program was very effective at preparing young men and women for the transitions they faced as they migrated from the world of college sports into their adult lives. It was so successful that it became a model for a national program that expanded to the athletic departments of more than 200 colleges and universities across the country. The Total Person Program was subsequently offered to all students at Georgia Tech. Will that program also expand to the full student bodies of other colleges and universities? We shall see!

During class, groups discussed compelling questions such as, "Which is more important, our willpower or our imagination?" The section about the human computer (Lesson One) helped to clear up this question. The students then wanted to know how society defines success. They concluded that success is the realization of a worthy idea, from attempt to completion. That led to a stimulating discussion about whether we should be considered failures for not living up to society's expectations. Life should not be viewed in terms of failure, we found, but in degrees of success.

SUCCESS is not a grand-slam homerun. Success is consistently hitting those dependable singles every day. Individual or groups that make it to the top concentrate on staying at bat and avoiding mistakes that detract from their performances. Once in a while, the perfect pitch comes across the plate. You will be ready to knock it out of the park if your hitting has been consistently solid.

The principle to grasp here is **PREPARATION**. Get ready for the big pitch by concentrating on singles until the right opportunity comes along. Ted Williams of the Boston Red Sox, the greatest hitter of all time, said that out of the twenty to fifty pitches that came his way every game, he expected only one perfect pitch. He had the self-discipline to wait and to be prepared when that pitch came.

A thin line divides success from failure. A determined person will not quit even in the darkest moment of tremendous strain. Training yourself to use your human computer to its fullest potential can propel you across that thin line, allowing you to make the jump from attempt to achievement.

PERCEPTION is another key to success. Many people live in an unreal world. They create a cosmos in their own minds based on the way they would like it to be, rather than the way it actually is. We must see the world of everyday life as it really is and know the difference between what is real and unreal, between fact and fiction, and between what works and what doesn't work. God has endowed us with a human computer that permeates our entire being and allows us to develop a clear and truthful perception.

There are four basic realities to understand:

1) We will always have **Problems**. If we don't, we have set our goals too low.

2) **There is a Natural Law of Balance**. We see it each day: electrons and protons; night and day; male and female; hot and cold; life and death; the two sides of a coin. Nothing is one way. For every positive, there's an offsetting negative; for every negative, there's an offsetting positive. To gain something, you must give up something. Always look quickly for the offsetting positive in every negative situation, which is what positive mental attitude is all about. Always look for the half-full glass rather than the half-empty glass. Look for the positives as soon as something goes wrong. This is a success force.

3) The **Law of Averages cannot be ignored**. Insurance companies use it to compile actuary tables. Gambling casinos use it to take your money. In sports we keep innumerable statistics. All things being equal, if you attempt something twenty times with the correct preparation, your chances of succeeding are twice as good as if you tried it only ten times. Why doesn't everybody apply this basic law? Most people do not believe the Law of Averages will work for them. Colonel Sanders approached more than a thousand restaurants before a single one bought his chicken recipe. Thomas Edison tried an immense number of techniques for creating a light bulb before he made any that worked. If we never quit, we will eventually succeed. We may

have temporary setbacks, but we will never be defeated.

4) Through the power of the mind, we can control our destiny. The principle of the **Subconscious Mind** – our subjective imagination, our human computer – will be thoroughly explained in a lesson to follow. Dr. Karl Pribram, a Stanford University neurosurgeon, has demonstrated convincingly the direct correlation between what the mind visualizes and what a person achieves. Develop the habit of imagining that you are already successful.

ATTITUDE should follow perception. After we comprehend that a situation is real, we need to position our minds for success. We can accomplish almost any task by applying a positive attitude, but a negative attitude will prevent us from succeeding. You've never seen a bookstore carry a title like *The Power of Negative Thinking*!

The American philosopher William James summed it up when he said, "The greatest revolution of our generation is the discovery that human beings, by changing the inner attitudes of their minds, can change the outer aspects of their lives." To acquire a true and positive mental attitude, we must analyze and understand exactly what a positive mental attitude is, and how and why it works.

CONCLUSION

The more positive your system of beliefs, the more you will believe in your ability to control your destiny. You will be able to accomplish specific tasks when others have said, "It can't be done."

Sometimes we may not get a solution that allows us to achieve our original objective. We may find an alternative that takes us in an entirely different direction. That direction more often than not turns out to be superior to the one in which we were originally headed.

WE ARE FREE TO CHOOSE OUR ATTITUDE

Can we motivate other people? We can help them to become motivated by guiding them to the source of their own power. Whether they move forward from there is a personal matter. Where is this power? It's inside everyone. It's the human computer, the starting place for developing positive and negative leadership.

We discovered in class discussion that an individual's personality is the sum total of all that person's habits and characteristics. Brainstorming, we came up with a list of positive words and phrases that describe a positive approach in an individual's personality. The positive leader often is most or all of the following:

- Trustworthy
- Moral
- Ethical
- A servant leader
- A leader by strong principles
- Unselfish
- Treats employees, followers, or customers with fairness
- Good listener and communicator
- Strong
- Friendly
- Uses common sense as necessary
- Positive
- Master of skills appropriate for a position
- Hard and smart worker
- Quick problem solver
- Master of tough decisions
- Has a vision for the company or program
- Surrounds himself/herself with positive and smart people
- Self motivated
- Effective leader

We usually find these types of leaders at the heads of nations, militaries, governments, corporations, companies, teams, religious organizations, medicine, education, families, and almost any field or group. Although styles may be different, in the final analysis, the positive leader has the best and sometimes the only chance to succeed.

By contrast, a negative leader may be some or all of these:

- Untrustworthy
- Immoral
- Unethical
- Corrupt
- Greedy
- Selfish
- Evil
- Poor communicator
- Unfair
- Negative
- Disloyal
- Weak
- Unfriendly
- Lazy
- Not respected by employees
- Surrounds himself/herself with people who can be controlled

During World War II (1941-1945), the media reported positively about America's involvement in the war to save the free world. We understood from reports in newspapers, in films, and on the radio that Germany and Japan had to be unconditionally defeated. As a seventeen-year-old young man, I wanted to join the military. The Navy admitted me and soon I began serving my country in the South Pacific theatre. Positive-ness was the key attitude that pulled everyone together. We were united.

During our class, a similar attitude developed. It's clear that being unified makes our nation stronger than the sum of its parts. Add to that our moral fiber and belief in God and His creation, and we have the foundation of strength that can overcome any obstacle. This program emphasizes how spirituality forms the base that we all work from to become a truly successful person, group or nation. Character, integrity, determination, and drive to overcome the many obstacles one may face are crucial for long-term success in sports, business, and in life! The power of prayer can enhance all of these things. God has given us the freedom to choose our own thoughts.

My friend Albert "Bud" Parker has been my close aide in directing the class through the many years. Each semester, I ask him to be one of the prestigious speakers who addresses the need for ethics in the business world. He always delivers a terrific message. This year he changed the angle of his topic and spoke about the 507th Parachute Infantry Regiment and its crucial contribution to winning World War II during the invasion of Normandy. Leaders come from all walks of life, and the military has produced its share of people whose personal sacrifices have paved the way for the freedoms that we all enjoy. In Appendix A, Bud shares the inspiring story of his father-in-law, an American paratrooper who contributed to the success of D-Day forces. Monique Gupta, a member of the 2003 Leadership Fitness class, adds her reflections after watching a film documenting the sacrifices of that regiment.

Especially in America, we have the freedom to choose how we experience life and its many opportunities. We can make those thoughts focus on prosperity, health, work and relationships. We are free to choose from the wonder of God's unlimited creation, the universe. In spirituality, people of all faiths – Christians, Jews, Muslims, Buddhists, and others – must respect each other's beliefs and communicate with each other to promote peace in the world. Otherwise the world will destroy itself. The more we bless others, the more God will bless us. Helping others and not dwelling on our own problems will multiply God's miracles and build bridges of understanding. The spirit of God within us gives us a vision that perceives the good that can become a reality. Before a great invention can take shape, someone with foresight and imagination steers it from idea to reality. That person unites spirit, mind, and body with God to form or create something. God is with us, as described in Acts 18:9-10. One night the Lord said to Paul in a vision, "Do not be afraid, but speak and do not be silent; for I am with you." God supplies the energy throughout our bodies to overcome any obstacle. He gives us vitality and strength of spirit, body, and mind. That mind is our human computer.

It is clear to all of us that the world today needs positive leaders. We have been shaken by numerous tragedies of late, from terrorism to corporate scandals. These issues make forming a positive plan even more important today.

This book builds a case for how to produce those positive leaders. *Leadership Fitness* will work for anyone, regardless of faith or career path. Whether used in education, religion, government, business, medicine, military, large groups, or small groups, *Leadership Fitness* presents a clear route to achieving that goal.

NOTE

Georgia Tech is a state-supported institution. This curriculum has been developed to demonstrate how I apply the principles of leadership fitness to my personal life. Where references to God, spirituality, and bible verses appear, one should understand that these are my personal opinions and beliefs. They do not reflect the individual views of class members or of the University. I encourage members of this class to apply the principles of leadership fitness to their own life perspectives. By integrating the lessons that follow into your own value system, you will gain the greatest amount from this course.

LESSON ONE

ARE YOU FIT TO BE A POSITIVE LEADER?

THE HUMAN COMPUTER

*You must **want** to become a positive leader,
and you must follow a plan of action
to become one.*

Positive leadership requires many elements. First, you must understand the intricacies of your position. You have to master knowledge, wisdom, fundamentals, strategies, techniques, and leadership nomenclature necessary for your situation. Then you have to be able to demonstrate, teach, and implement these requirements. Finally, you must provide the positive leadership that will produce success. Are you fit to be a positive leader?

A positive leader will guide the members of his or her team to a resource that will empower and motivate them to success. Leaders come in all types, however, and some are evil, corrupt, greedy, selfish, or untrustworthy. These types are capable of generating successful results, but at some point in time, they will fail miserably. Their demise can harm people severely, causing teams, corporations, or even governments to break down.

The *Leadership Fitness* plan focuses on the positive person who is trustworthy. That leader is strong, unselfish, fair, friendly, and has both common sense and excellent communication skills. These traits gain respect from employees and make a leader known as a giver rather than a taker. With these characteristics, you can train yourself and then those around you to be capable of mentally motivating themselves. This internal drive is the difference between winning and losing, between success and failure. But first you, the leader, must become that self-motivated person.

Let's explore the facts. A person who is self-motivated is prepared to understand the mental element of life. We have resources within us that provide the power to do practically anything. Belief is the way of focusing our power onto a goal. To realize our beliefs, we need to exercise several principles. We must understand the functions of our brain, part of which operates at the sub-conscious level. Like a computer, that segment operates as an information processing mechanism. That computer, and hence our attitudes, can be changed and improved by our actions. Each of us can develop a technique that gives us full access to and control over our built-in personal computer.

Understanding our brain allows us to control and use its power. Having this power at our disposal can motivate us, energize us and give us control over how we intentionally behave to reach specific goals. Computers compile, sort, and correlate data, solving problems by virtue of how they respond to input and output. Input refers to information inserted into the machine. That information is converted into a code. The computer processes and acts upon that information in accordance with instructions and other information that make up the program. The resulting information, returned to the user through a paper printout or on a display screen, is known as output.

Human memory works the same as any manufactured computer. Input enters our brains in the form of information. We process that information through a variety of programs that we carry within us. Those programs are diverse, and they include sophisticated ways of thinking or behaving that we have picked up through a lifetime of experience. Processing input through those mental codes results in the output – the actions we take, conclusions we draw, and emotions we feel. Human beings are programmed much the same as man-made computers: input, instructions, information sorting, and output.

Randall W. Engle, research scientist and chair of the School of Psychology in the College of Sciences at Georgia Tech, recently explained how performance on measurements of working memory capacity predicts performance on a wide range of real-world cognitive tasks. In other words, we have the ability to focus on a task and block out other distractions. The objective imagination of our conscious mind can control our thoughts for either positive or negative results.

The human brain weighs about fifty ounces, or just over three pounds. It is comprised of tens of billions of nerve cells. Computer chips would have to be at least 10,000 times larger than their current capacity to approach that number. Think of this incredible source of power that each of us is blessed with. That power came to us as a gift from God. Our responsibility, in return, is to thank Him for this gift and to use it for worthwhile achievements, and after achieving success, to thank Him again.

The brain has two minds: the conscious and the subconscious. The conscious mind accepts our thoughts and passes the information on to the subconscious, which records, sorts, and produces our thoughts. I call this the human computer because of its similar functions to the manufactured computers we use every day. This process is the key determinant of the actions that we will take.

There is a simple secret that makes this computer analogy valuable. By controlling what comes into your conscious mind, you can influence your own actions. If a thought is negative, unworthy, evil or corrupt, stop for one full minute and change that thought into a positive, worthwhile one. By practicing this action over a period of time, you can become the person and leader you aspire to be. This process is the Attitude Technique. By learning this lesson and passing it on to our followers, we will spark motivation for success throughout our team. Through years of research, study and moment-by-moment practice, I have developed a philosophy from this concept that has literally changed people's lives – including my own – for the better.

This is the source of true motivation. The human computer accepts as input whatever the conscious mind allows it to receive. Our subconscious does not know the difference between what is real and what is imagined; it only processes the input passed to it from the objective imagination. Give it clean, wholesome and positive information, and you will act as a person motivated by those traits. Convey this to your team, and they, in turn, will become believers and winners.

A magnetized piece of steel will lift twelve times its own weight, but if you demagnetize the same piece of steel it will not even lift a feather. Similarly, there are two types of people – the magnetized person, who is full of confidence and faith, and the demagnetized type, who is full of fears and doubt. When opportunities come, the demagnetized person says, "I might fail." And failure will come because his or her human computer has been instructed to execute those thoughts. By absorbing and teaching the Attitude Technique philosophy, we can change the negative to the positive, and bad to good, through self-motivating actions that will produce successful results. Our imagination is stronger than our willpower – if it is directed through the human computer.

The practice of the Attitude Technique will undoubtedly produce positive results. Ralph Waldo Emerson said, "Man is what he thinks all day long." William James, the father of American psychology, said, "The power to move the world is in your sub-conscious mind." And the Bible says, "If you believe, you will receive whatever you ask for in prayer." (Matthew 21:22) We literally become what we think about and plan. By repeating positive affirmations over and over again, we ensure that our sub-conscious, or subjective imagination, accepts this as real and performs positive actions. We bring things into being through self-imaging.

Careful planning is important to success. You have probably heard the story of the two men hiking in the Rocky Mountains when they see a grizzly bear in the distance coming toward them. Immediately, one of the men pulls his running shoes out of his backpack and begins putting them on. The other man looks at him and says, "You know you can't outrun the grizzly." The first man replies, "I don't have to. I just have to outrun you." For the game of life, we need a game plan. Do you have a plan for your life and for your leadership role?

Once we get our own thinking straight, we are ready to teach our staff or team members the simple secret. We then can set goals both for our personal life and for the organization.

Positive attitudes lead people to the winner's circle in all areas of life. All of us experience problems or troubles in life. But more important than the difficulties is how we react to them. People who have positive attitudes still face disappointments, frustrations, and pressures, but their reactions are different. Problems can cause unhappiness, and they can defeat you if you allow that to happen. But if you never give up, you will eventually win!

We may experience temporary defeat, but if we persevere, we will win. Babe Ruth struck out more times than any man in baseball history. Ty Cobb was thrown out trying to steal more than any man in baseball history. Jackie Robinson overcame mental and physical abuse to become the first African-American to play Major League Baseball. Vince Lombardi, one of the most successful football coaches of his time, was line coach at Fordham University at age 43. His great success came years later. Paul Brown, a man who coached successfully at all levels of football – from high school to college, from military to professional – had many setbacks. But his will was stronger than any temporary defeat.

Albert Einstein flunked courses in math. Henry Ford was broke at age 40. Andrew Young, a frequent speaker to my Leadership Fitness classes, overcame racial discrimination to become the United States' representative to the United Nations. Thomas Edison's teacher called him a dunce, and Edison later failed more than 14,000 times in his efforts to perfect the incandescent light. I have seen many athletes become stars who once could not make the team – even some who were advised to drop out of their sport. Archie Griffin was told he was too small to play football on the college level, let alone at powerhouse Ohio State; "You'll never play. You'll be lost in the shuffle," critics said. But Archie not only played, he became the only two-time Heisman Trophy winner in history. Later on, I was fortunate to coach Archie as a productive running back with the NFL Cincinnati Bengals. The examples go on and on. The lesson to learn is that we are created for a purpose. You are here for a reason. You only need a direction. The Attitude Technique philosophy will lead you to become whatever you desire to become.

As you set your goals, first of all, think wisely. "What do I have, and what can I do with what I have in order to reach where I want to go?" Put your goals into writing. When a goal is written, it is crystallized. You know exactly what you want to do. Booker T. Washington said, "I have begun everything with the idea that I could succeed." Committing your goal to paper impresses it upon the subconscious mind. This will guide the human computer to work 24 hours each day to reach your desire. If you plan wisely, if you do it step-by-step as you experience similar successes on the way toward ultimate success, good things will happen because you will make them happen. Remember: A winner is always aware of what he or she doesn't know, and works to improve in those areas.

As leaders, we can make a difference in the future of our countries by becoming self-motivated positive leaders for the betterment of mankind and passing on to our followers the proper use of a powerful tool – our human computer. In my own search for a higher goal, I often use the Bible. For me, God is the source for all our needs. The seventh chapter of Matthew, seventh and eighth verses, offer the familiar words, "Ask and you will be given what you ask for. Seek and you will find. Knock and the door will be opened. For everyone who asks, receives. Anyone who seeks, finds. If only you will knock, the door will be opened." (*The Living Bible.*)

An organization that is making a difference on college campuses across the country is Omicron Delta Kappa Society (ODK). Students, faculty, administration are recognized for their positive leadership. I asked my friend John Morgan, Executive Director of the Omicron Delta Kappa Society, to share the ODK Leadership Development Program (Appendix B).

You may decide to stay right where you are and to make your job and your life meaningful and successful. You may decide you want to move to a higher or different position in another location. Whatever path you decide upon can become a happy, exciting adventure. You don't need to delay or hold off. Start now – the rewards are waiting for you. The architect of the universe did not design a ladder leading nowhere. The carpenter from the plains of Galilee gave us the only tool we need – the advice of his teaching: "As you sow, so shall you reap." We become what we plan. We are at this moment exactly what we have planned to be: nothing more, nothing less. All the philosophers, prophets, teachers and wise men throughout history have disagreed on many things, but on this one subject they are in complete and unanimous agreement. Marcus Aurelius, the great Roman emperor and philosopher, said, " A man's life is what his thoughts are made of." In more modern times, Dr. Norman Vincent Peal said, "If we think in negative terms, we receive negative results. Conversely, if we think in positive terms, we receive the positive results." We can control our lives by controlling our thoughts. Remember: We become what we plan. This is the human computer in action.

I have applied this principle first to my life and then to the young men I have coached. Through writing and public speaking, I have shared it with thousands of others. It all began when I realized that it was possible to reach positive success in any task I decided to undertake, whether in education, coaching, administration or business – with the right approach.

As the years passed, there were times when my control seemed less strong or in doubt. Those were the moments when I simply reread, restudied, and readjusted to regain my objective and subjective thinking with the practice of the Attitude Technique. Each and every time, this set me back on the right track.

The Attitude Technique might be considered a success force. As my life continued through the years, I sometimes realized that I was slipping downward. At those times a force of energy caught me, as if to remind me of the direction I had set. This energized me to put my force into forward motion again, and to apply the technique to regain a forward and upward path. It always worked.

This is an affirmative, scientific approach to becoming a winner – a complete winner. Your future will result from your plan. It is difficult to predict the future. Problems will always exist in the world, and predicting the future is presumptuous. Nevertheless, a positive, planned, personal program is still clearly necessary and viable. A person can control his or her future. Success can be yours as it has been for others. Striving to become the successful, positive leader of the organization or a small group can be the most exciting adventure you will ever undertake.

A true positive leader brings people together for the common goal of achieving positive success. This type of leadership unites; it does not divide. United we stand – divided we fall! Once you have begun practicing self-motivation through using your human computer, other people will notice. They will want to be around you. And they will follow you.

What better time to exercise this achievement than now, when the world needs our positive-ness more than ever before?. Everyone wins!

KEEPING SCORE

Before moving on to Lesson Two, rate your assets (strengths) and liabilities (weaknesses). Darrell Royal, a famous University of Texas football coach, once made the statement, "If the game isn't important, why do we keep score?" In other words, it is important to keep score in order to decide who wins and who loses. The same applies in life. Are we winners or losers? If your life is important, then we should keep score!

The Keeping Score chart must be filled in for you to see where you stand. After you complete the nine lessons, you will be asked to score yourself again. You should work on this process throughout your life, not just in this class. The feedback you will gain from this exercise will help you change liabilities (weaknesses) into assets (strengths).

KEEPING SCORE

Rate: Superior, Excellent, Good, Fair, or Poor
Then Go Back and Write in Your Remarks

Subject	Assets (Strengths)	Liabilities (Weaknesses)
Spiritual Values		
Family Relations		
How I Perceive Myself		
How I Think Others Perceive Me		
Social Life		
How I Get Along With Others		
Health Status		
Aerobic Fitness		

Subject	Assets (Strengths)	Liabilities (Weaknesses)
Relaxation		
Recreational		
Rest		
Mental Stimulation		
Self-Discipline		
Self-Motivation		
Self-Confidence		
Controlled Visualization		
Goal Setting		
Career		
Financial Planning		

LESSON TWO

THE BIRTH AND DEVELOPMENT OF THE ATTITUDE TECHNIQUE PHILOSOPHY

A TOTAL PERSON-TOTAL SUCCESS CONCEPT

People continue to ask me, "Where and how did the Attitude Technique begin?" My answer is always the same. For my twelfth birthday in 1939, my father presented me with a book entitled *I Dare You*. That book by William Danforth, chairman of the Checker Board Square in St. Louis, MO, was one of the first books written on goal setting. This masterpiece challenged me to spend effort considering how I approached life. It stimulated me to search for the secrets to successful living. The book instructed readers to write goals in every area of their lives. I began this "dare." Throughout the years, each goal I have written has come true. This made it simple for me to become a believer in the practice of setting to paper the things I wanted to achieve.

Later on, when I entered my career as a high school coach, I began using the term Attitude Technique. I don't remember the exact time and place, but the basis was this: in our coaching drills we referred to various methods of teaching each player skills in his position. These were physical techniques. Realizing there must be a mental skill to initiate each physical practice, I at first called this "the mental technique." A player's thoughts must be perfected before he can carry out his assignments. I later changed the word mental to "attitude," thus resulting in the Attitude Technique.

There are many degrees of attitude, so excelling at the process required further analysis. I knew that attitude had to be positive to produce successful results. Then my curiosity, study, and research moved toward finding a simple way to develop and maintain a positive attitude. While some people may be more optimistic than others by nature, I discovered a specific technique for developing optimism in oneself. I found that secret, and I have used it throughout my life and career. As positive results occurred, I began sharing the system with others – with my family, my teams, in seminars and workshops, in articles, and through books. The feedback was unbelievably positive. Because of that response, the Attitude Technique philosophy became my high purpose in life, and sharing it became my goal. Through the years, I worked on this personal project almost daily despite ups and downs, victories and defeats, good times and tough times. Nevertheless, the Attitude Technique program kept me going. Here's my story.

My career started as a high school coach in a small, rural area. During my initial season, only seven players reported to the first practice. I will never forget running all the way home (we did not own an automobile at the time) shortly before the first game and hugging my wife Phyllis with joy because the eleventh player had finally reported. I finally had enough players to start the first game. That was a special team. We were united to do our very best. And they succeeded, accomplishing an undefeated season – the only one in the school's history. They followed instructions perfectly, and that year jumpstarted my career as a football coach, providing me with self-confidence. The positive approach actually worked. However, to follow up I needed more study, more information—so the story continues.

During the early years of my career, I needed to take an additional job to supplement my income. I accepted a part-time position with a life insurance company. During a sales program, I learned the basic principles of management and motivation. Before six months had elapsed, I led the company in sales. In fact, the insurance job potential was so lucrative that I soon faced the difficult decision of which career path I wanted to follow – professional sales or athletics. I now know that the program I developed would have allowed me to be successful in any profession. By faithfully practicing the Attitude Technique philosophy, I advanced from that first, small high school to a prominent, larger one, then to the college ranks, on to the National Football League, and finally to positions as the director of athletics and executive assistant to the president at two of the leading universities in the nation. This trajectory did not come by accident. It was planned. I trained myself, and I was prepared for each opportunity when it came.

It's impossible not to notice that as I write this narrative, the personal pronoun "I" appears frequently. That's because it is imperative for me to show how the Attitude Technique lessons have worked in my own life in order for you, the reader, to embark upon your own successful path to positive success. I believe strongly in the team system – a united group working together for a common cause, finishing with a victory. But the leader, who has the ultimate responsibility, stands alone. That person must be a positive force.

The word positive has many meanings: confident, certain, affirmative, among others. In this book, positive means the ultimate form of worthiness, goodness, ability to inspire trust, and many other qualities that represent what is *good*. The positive leader is fit, on many levels, to be the ultimate person in charge.

Utilizing written goals and plans, I found it possible to achieve exactly what I wanted. The results have been amazing. More importantly, while finding the pathway for my own journey, I developed a program that could be shared with others. What are these management and motivation principles that I learned and practiced? During the early 1950s, top executives of large corporations studied the scientific basis of success. The private sessions and seminars they sponsored yielded spectacular results, but the findings were kept secret until companies specializing in teaching motivation began to merchandise the information. The material then became available to anyone. Only a few took advantage, however.

In the life insurance field, I was introduced to motivational material for business executives. Along with reading the book *I Dare You*, I began studying, researching and applying those corporate principles to my life and work. To completely understand the management concept, I began translating the executive language into everyday lessons. Little by little, I developed a guide that produced almost unbelievable results.

As I continued my studies, I wondered why some people were successful and others were not. My curiosity about this was keen. I wanted to understand why and how successful people got where they were. At first most of my concern revolved around the field of athletics. Why were certain athletes better than others? When I myself was a young athlete before my work career began, I had sought out ways to become a better player. This desire to understand the nature of achievement continued as I grew older. During my college years, I read anything I could find that dealt with success and motivation. The works of Andrew Carnegie were among the first I came across. Later on, someone gave me the book *Think and Grow Rich* by Napoleon Hill. From it I learned to rank the ideas that I could use to challenge myself in my pursuit.

When I began my coaching career on the high school level in 1951, my inquisitiveness was even stronger. I made a trip to Massillon, OH. At that time Massillon High School was considered the best high school football team in the nation. After going over their program from top to bottom, I realized they were winning because of one thing – a planned positive attitude. They actually believed they would win each and every contest. That made an indelible impression upon me. Shortly after my return from Massillon, I listened to a record by Earl Nightingale titled, "The Strangest Secret." It wrapped up the works of Andrew Carnegie, Napoleon Hill, and Norman Vincent Peale all in one package. It was inspiring and led me to read Peale's works: *The Art of Living*, *The Power of Positive Thinking*, and *The Amazing Results of Positive Thinking*. I analyzed Dr. Peale's Philosophy and integrated it into my own.

Later I met Paul J. Meyer, founder and president of Success Motivation® Institute. He encouraged me to further my study in the field. I began taking the management and goal-setting courses offered by his company. I started early each morning and studied for only thirty minutes, but it was worth every minute. In just thirty minutes a day, I gained something that probably has made the difference in my life today: I developed an attitude with which to start the day, direct my thoughts, and eventually control my life. I went through several cassette tape programs offered by Paul Meyer's company. They were sensational. Each tape emphasized space repetition. Each time I listened to the tape and read the text simultaneously, I received an idea that I could incorporate into my work that particular day. The idea was always a positive, worthwhile gesture that facilitated progress in some area. When you begin to add up one idea each day, you can see how the suggestions multiplied and amazing results began to flow.

With an enthusiasm that seemed inspired, I continued to read other books throughout the early years: *The Magic of Thinking*

Big by David J. Schwartz; *Psycho Cybernetics* by Maxwell Maltz; *On Becoming Human* by Ross Snyder; *Life is Tremendous* by Charles E. Jones; *Secrets of Mind Power* by Harry Lorayne; *Successful Living* by Nelson Boswell; *The Magic of Believing* by Claude M. Bristol; *You Can Become the Person You Want to Be* by Robert H. Schuller; *As a Man Thinketh* by James Allen; *The Success System That Never Fails* by Clement Stone; *The Greatest Salesman in the World* by Og Mandino; *See You at the Top* by Zig Ziglar; *The Blueprint* by Carl Stevens; *Positive Books* by Jack Kinder; and hundreds of additional books on the subject of success. As the years passed, each book contributed to my thinking. I researched and digested them until I adopted their common tenet: "Control your mind and, in turn, control your life in a positive mental attitude."

After I began my personal program, I wanted to test the technique on young men in athletics. With my advanced research and my own work in athletics, the stage was set for me to apply success theories to a particular football coaching situation. The experiment would be a live test because the result would be judged by thousands of people and measured by the direct effect it had on members of the squad.

My first attempts were a bit discouraging, and it would have been easy to be cynical and give up. I had learned that most people do not take full advantage of their opportunities in our country.. Despite the fact that the United States is the richest land on the face of the earth, only about five to ten percent ever achieve complete success. Why is this?

The secret of all successful people starts with setting a predetermined goal. The fact that the odds may be as high as ninety-five percent against a person's becoming successful means that the field is wide open for those with the desire to achieve their goals. The potential is present in each of us, and we only have to know how simple it is to use our valuable resources. The great majority of people don't even try, however. Only one in one thousand will thoroughly attempt this plan. Will I be that one, I wondered? I was recommitted.

Anyone can reach a plateau of mediocrity, but achievers will decide how high above that plateau they want to rise by setting goals. The amount of success a person achieves is the direct result of how well he or she plans each and every moment. So long as the thinking is good, worthy, and clearly defined in the mind, the individual is on the way to some very satisfying experiences — on the way, in fact, to total success.

Each goal must be a simple ambition without other complications. This literally means that you must decide what you want in life. The goal must fit into a plan and be something to bounce out of bed for every morning. And you have to set your sights high. Thinking big creates its own magic. It is absolutely necessary to reach for the sky and to command all the resources available.

This means we have to have a commitment: What do we want? We must then decide when we want to reach our goal and determine the ingredients necessary to achieving that goal. Follow that with an assessment of what we are willing to give in return for what we will receive. The final step is self-imagery: Visualize the goal already accomplished and start believing it will come about. With this formula, you can use the power of positive prayer by asking God to guide you toward your worthy goal.

Write these steps and read them aloud each day. This brings about the action component. We can plan a lot of things, but unless we act upon them, our total efforts will fall hard and fast. After the plan works the first time, we begin expecting it to succeed each time.

As we control our thinking in a positive and worthwhile manner, we can achieve whatever we want. If our thoughts become negative, we will have negative problems. It means starting over again until we learn to accept and believe.

In my first application of the Attitude Technique, I asked each member of the squad to work out his personal plan for life. Then we set our goal for the football season. Our goal was to establish the best record in the history of the school. We made the plan. Then we began the action.

It wasn't easy, but the Attitude Technique soon caused changes in the lives of our players. Very few people really believed we would achieve the success we were shooting for, because not many people understood our plan. It was our secret, and we had pledged not to reveal our team goal to anyone outside the squad family. As the season opened that year, we had no doubt in our minds that we would play each and every minute with the precision of the plan. We thought of each member as a link in a chain. A single link doubting our goal could break the chain. Each member of the squad became very important. This put tremendous responsibility on each person, for the failure of one jeopardized the organization's success. Our plan involved the entire squad, not just the first eleven, demanding a strong sense of dedication and concentration.

After the first game, the final score indicated that our plan would work. This was a great feeling. Our season had a fine start, but the battle had only begun. We realized that to continue, we had to improve each day. This is the essence of motivation – growing as an individual and improving as a player each day. It is a plain fact in any test of skills that we are either getting better or slipping backwards. We never stand still. After a single accomplishment, it is common to let up on a large goal. That's how upsets happen in sports. Our team had taken the first step. Now it was time to dig in and work even harder to prepare for the coming opponent. During the next week, we worked for improvement. Each day we strove to be just a little bit better than the day before. We knew we had to do this to accomplish our task, and that we had undertaken a continuing process.

Although the first season started fine, it had downturns. At times we were frustrated, fearful, and worried. Several players developed a negative attitude. A number quit the squad – not because of the hard physical work, but because they would not allow themselves to accept the positive mental attitude each individual had to assume to succeed in our undertaking.

The practice of controlled thinking sometimes reminds me of an illustration. If you placed an iron plank six inches wide and fifty feet long on the ground, anyone could walk its length without difficulty. But place the same plank a hundred feet up in the air, braced between two buildings and over a street, and hardly anyone would ever attempt to cross it. And why is that? The plank is the same, whether lying on the ground or as a bridge across a street. The people who walk its length on the ground have the same muscles, the same mind, and the same will. But the person who sees the board suspended in mid-air typically thinks about falling. Great leadership is the capacity to develop the will to achieve and accept a positive mental attitude toward the attempt, rather than focusing on failure.

The next season brought back several young men who were dedicated in their willingness to think positively. We also gained several new players who were ready to learn. It was a fresh year. We capitalized on the mistakes, trials, and tribulations of the past season and once again started our work for the new season in the same manner as the previous year. However, we worked and thought positively even more than before. The season rolled on. When it was completed, we found ourselves just one point and 30 seconds short of our goal. Although we had not reached the perfect season, we had had the best season yet. This proved to the players and coaching staff that our goal could be obtained. It truly was possible. We were becoming believers.

All we needed was just a little more effort. We had come so close to our goal, yet hardly anyone was satisfied because we realized we could have made it if only we had believed strongly enough. The chain, with each of us as a durable link, was forming and becoming stronger. When the following year arrived, our athletes were ready. They had talked about their intentions with one another, and they had worked very hard over the summer to be in the best physical condition possible. When fall practice opened, these players were not going to be denied their victory. The parked their automobiles and began riding bicycles. They were off the streets at 8:30 p.m. and in bed each night by 10:30, living the life of a true athlete.

The chief of police remarked to me the effect this program had on the entire community. He related how peaceful his job became when football season began. When classes opened, our players were leaders. Many of our young men held offices in their classrooms and in student government. They not only went to church each week, but they also influenced their parents to go. This squad had found the key and gone to work.

That year we became the state champions. We achieved that best season. The squad received numerous accolades. While they were flushed with this success, I took the opportunity to remind them that this was just the first step toward a complete life of success. They had accomplished their goal as a result of their planning. They had simply decided to be something in life. The ones who stayed with it realized fully that they could continue and achieve their life ambitions. They understood the secret. And it was so simple.

Why only a few actually make the grade is difficult to understand. We can stumble around as we attempt success, but if we never pinpoint our objectives, we will allow negative thoughts to creep in and we will give up easily. An individual finds out about himself or herself through participating in sports. He or she learns to win the battle over self, to submit to self-discipline, and to believe.

This approach to football for the high school team was amazing. It brought about a season considered the best in the school's history and a claim to the state championship. Remember, however, that this did not happen in the first season or even in the second.,. It happened in the third season, when it was clear that the staff and players would not quit. They persevered and became true winners. After that remarkable year, could the program stay on top? Could it improve? The first players would be graduating and new young men taking their places. The Attitude Technique still existed. And the graduating seniors had planned beyond the football season. Their careers for life had been designed. They carried with them the benefits of what they had learned and, in addition, built the foundation for those who came after them. It was always an exceptional experience for me to follow their budding careers, which made me realize even more that this program works!

The "program," as it was often called, was highly respected in our area and gained prominence in other places. I was asked to lecture at many clinics and to write articles on our football techniques for national sports magazines. Attendance at our games began to soar. An undefeated regular season carried through to fifty consecutive victories. It wasn't easy, but the next four seasons each produced championships. Each year critics predicted the fall of the empire, but we confounded skeptics by repeating the previous year's success. The new team not only believed they could win but they also expected victory – and they won!

Looking back to that first year, I can see it would have been easy to give up on our goal. Sometimes we nearly did. There were frustrating moments, just as in any climb to gain excellence. But we knew we would never find out what lay inside of us if we did not strive to do our best and then some. At times we held on by only a thread. But we proved that we had to hang on together in order to regain the momentum to carry us to the top. Each contest in life must be approached this way.

In sports, there comes a time when one team experiences frustrations and the members have to decide whether they will give up. At that moment, the opposing team finds it easy to take control and claim victory. But if we hang on, never lose our composure, and strive for excellence even through the darkest moments, we can win. It may take until the last second, but even that final part of the contest is what we must prepare for. We are in it for the entire game – for an entire life.

You must be a giver. A person gets back from life what he or she puts into it. In business, a person's earnings are measured by service. To earn money we must provide more and better service. Conversely, earnings will fall if we give poor service. This principle holds in every form of human endeavor: it is true in our spiritual life, in marriage, in athletics, in business, in everything. The return is in proportion to the personal investment.

My test with this particular high school football program proved that the Attitude Technique theory was valid. Each player now had the chief ingredient to become successful in his coming life. He understood it was easy to reach success by following this plan. Yet at least 90 percent of people do not apply themselves fully to reaching their goals, leaving the field wide open for those who will.

This experience was only one example, but it inspired me to continue the study and research of the mental principles that ensure happiness, fulfillment, and achievement. I learned that a person cannot be forced to do something he or she is not willing to do voluntarily. The way to get people to choose success is by understanding that they respond to challenges and quality leadership. People can be stimulated by fear and incentives, but their responses will not be consistent or permanent. Each person emotionally responds to commands with either gratitude or resentment. Attitude creates a personal and effective motivation that can be accomplished only on an individual basis.

As the years passed, the Attitude Technique philosophy came to be utilized numerous times. Given enough time to be implemented, the plan never failed.

What I am talking about, and the ultimate objective of the philosophy, is having a winning career, living a vibrant life, developing inner happiness, and retiring financially independent. As you will see, the Attitude Technique can lead to a complete life.

The following chapters will spell out the steps to total success. As a positive leader, you will be energized to jump up and move forward!

LESSON THREE

TIME MANAGEMENT
PLANNING OUR THOUGHTS

Warning!
Lack of planning may be hazardous to your future!

~

The bad news is time flies. The good news is you're the pilot.
— Michael Altshuler

~

In coaching, it is important to have a game plan
for each game. However, it's more important
to have a game plan for your life!

To become a positive, successful person who leads a group, one must be highly organized. We control our lives by scheduling our time. Efficiency is the result of attention to detail. To become an effective leader, the first step is to manage your time well.

In my early years, I struggled with details and working out time schedules. After studying Paul Meyer's Success Motivation® program, I learned to organize my time to become effective as a leader. Later on I was tested on the "right brain-left brain" theory. I turned out to be a big picture person – a visionary. That's why I had difficulty with the details of time. By utilizing the time study program,

I learned to excel in both the large picture and the details.

Before we move on, it is important to write down your thoughts. This program is about you. Start by writing the thoughts that will shape your life and future. Those thoughts precede our ability to schedule time properly. In order to lead others, you first must become the person you want to be. The following charts will help you define your goals.

MASTER DREAM LIST

Write everything you've ever wanted, every place you've wanted to go, and everything you'd like to become or achieve. Date each item when you enter it.

In compiling the list below, remember to take off the judge's robe and let your imagination run free. Give no consideration to limitations, money, education, ability, or what may seem illogical. This is a completely unrestrained list.

_____

_____

_____

_____

_____

_____

_____

_____

_____

_____

_____

_____

_____

_____

_____

_____

_____

_____

_____

_____

_____

_____

_____

_____

_____

_____

_____

_____

The Master Dream List is an important exercise in seeking your goals. This is *where* and *how* starts. Don't hold back. Let the human computer explore all avenues. And remember, the subconscious mind (human computer) does not distinguish between what is objective and subjective. It will record whatever your conscious thoughts feed to your subconscious mind. By writing these thoughts into the master dream list, you are actually applying another sense to your memory bank.

We learn and comprehend by way of our five senses: sight, smell, hearing, speech, and touch. The more senses we use at one time, the more we comprehend. By writing our thoughts on the Master Dream List, then reading them aloud to send that information to the brain, we have exercised multiple senses for recording those thoughts.

After working with the Master Dream List for several days, turn to the next chart, "Where I Stand in My Present Job." A top leader should know exactly where he or she stands. You may be an employee or staff member without leadership responsibilities but aspire to move in that direction. You may already possess a high leadership position but need to improve by understanding the qualities necessary for attaining that goal, wherever you rank on the scale. Begin by describing your professional status.

Once you have a good start on where you currently stand, turn to the next chart, "Where I Want To Go in My Profession." Perhaps you may want to stay exactly where you are. But if you see yourself moving up the ladder of success to a more demanding and rewarding position, this chart will prepare you for your future climb.

WHERE I STAND IN MY PRESENT CAREER

Your description of your present professional status should include a list of your strengths, talents, abilities, and accomplishments, as well as your weaknesses and needs. Rewrite the description when significant change or personal growth occurs.

Date: _____

_____

_____

_____

_____

_____

_____

_____

_____

_____
_____
_____
_____
_____
_____
_____
_____
_____
_____
_____
_____
_____
_____
_____
_____
_____
_____
_____

WHERE I WANT TO GO IN MY PROFESSION

Make your description specific. Include exact duties, type of
organization, and details of the position you desire.

Date: _____

_____
_____
_____
_____
_____

_____

_____

_____

_____

_____

_____

_____

_____

_____

_____

_____

_____

_____

_____

_____

_____

_____

_____

_____

How do we build a successful and happy life? Thomas Edison once said, "Genius is one percent inspiration and ninety-nine percent perspiration." It is certainly true that fortune favors the prepared.

Time is our most valuable possession. Proper time control motivates us to succeed. How you use each moment will determine how far you climb in any area.

Nature's treasures can be tapped easily if you understand how to use your time intelligently. Remember: once we waste time, it is gone forever and can never be replaced. Each day is of the highest importance because we exchange one day of our lives for it. With each day that passes, we are running out of time. The wasted hours you spend are the very ones that you could have used constructively to win victory.

Use your time wisely and you will be repaid in multiples. Bob Richards, the former Olympic pole vault champion, began the groundwork for his future success at age thirteen. From that age, he spent more than 10,000 hours in preparation for his event, with the result that he became a world champion. Wisely invest 10,000 hours into any task, and you will become the champion of what you desire.

Time control, planning, and motivation are closely related. Motivation is planning – planning your career and your life. Planning does not mean daydreaming. It means written planning, or setting up the design in advance – for one year, one month, one week, or one day.

Write a daily plan to follow. By following it, you develop the self-discipline necessary to become motivated.

How does one organize time? First you must find out how you are presently using your time. You are going to be surprised. We often say, "If only I had more time," or, "I just can't do it – I don't have the time." But when you discover how you are using your precious time … well, get ready for some fun!

For starters, list in descending order on Your Task List everything in which you are involved. Each of us has different responsibilities, activities, and everyday duties. Some of the differences are slight; others are substantial. There is no typical example, but as an illustration, I have indicated on the following chart my own list from when I was a NFL head football coach. I call it a task list. It includes an outline of the demands upon my time during that period of my career, including my personal life, my civic life, my church life, and the responsibilities of my position.

TASK LIST (EXAMPLE)

1. Major goals for team and plans to accomplish these goals
2. Structuring of program to achieve top performance
3. Organization and management of staff
4. Out-of-season, in-season fitness program
5. Technical aspects of the game (film study)
6. Motivation program for staff and players
7. Scouting service and preparation for the college player draft
8. Public relations for club
9. Leadership program – "Attitude Technique, Inc."
10. Staff personnel selections
11. Calendar planning
12. Daily correspondence
13. Everyday folder
14. Meetings involving league
15. Speaking engagements
16. Individual conferences and letter writing to players
17. Personal fitness and recreation activities
18. Bible study, prayer, and meditation
19. Personal goals
20. Family activities
21. Civic, charitable, and national organizations
22. Reading
23. Writing
24. Meals, personal hygiene
25. Telephone
26. Interruptions
27.
28.
29.
30.
31.

YOUR TASK LIST

1.
2.
3.
4.
5.
6.
7.
8.
9.
10.
11.
12.
13.
14.
15.
16.
17.
18.
19.
20.
21.
22.
23.
24.
25.
26.
27.
28.
29.
30.
31.

I listed twenty-six items on my task list. I also left plenty of open spaces at the end because I know from experience that as I review the list, I will become aware of tasks not listed that I didn't realize I was doing.

Once you have made a list of everything you think you are involved in, break your day into three parts—morning, afternoon, and evening. Then divide your tasks among these sections. This is the basic document for a "test of time."

Next, start recording each day from the moment you wake up. Record the minutes you are actually engaged in an activity (no matter what it is) under the hour it occurs. When the day is over, total the number of minutes. You will discover how much time you are spending on each item on your Time Task list. No matter how thorough you believe your list to be, it is likely that other responsibilities, activities, and surprises will arise that you did not anticipate. Be sure to list telephone calls and interruptions on your task list. They consume an inordinate amount of time. When I first used the "Test of Time," I found I was allowing the telephone and other interruptions to rule my day. At first you may forget to record certain elements, but stay with it for one full week to get a good test.

Once you find out where your time is going, you can begin to work out plans to use your minutes and hours in a productive manner.

TIME STUDY ANALYSIS

DATE _____

TASK LIST	MORNING						AFTERNOON						EVENING						TOTAL MINUTES
	6	7	8	9	10	11	12	1	2	3	4	5	6	7	8	9	10	11	
1.																			
2.																			
3.																			
4.																			
5.																			
6.																			
7.																			
8.																			
9.																			
10.																			
11.																			
12.																			
13.																			
14.																			
15.																			
16.																			
17.																			
18.																			
19.																			
20.																			
21.																			

TASK LIST	MORNING						AFTERNOON						EVENING						TOTAL MINUTES
	6	7	8	9	10	11	12	1	2	3	4	5	6	7	8	9	10	11	
22.																			
23.																			
24.																			
25.																			
26.																			
27.																			
28.																			
29.																			
30.																			
31.																			
32.																			
33.																			
34.																			
35.																			
36.																			
37.																			
38.																			
39.																			
40.																			
41.																			
42.																			

After completing and analyzing the "Test of Time," begin writing a basic plan to follow. First list the standard procedures you need to follow each day. If you maintain an office as an administrator, consider these eight items to be checked every day:

- Everyday folder (keep current items available)
- Meetings (time)
- Appointments (time)
- Correspondence (in and out)
- Planning sessions
- Telephone messages
- Other details and surprises
- Interruptions (record and learn how to reduce this number)

If you have a secretary or personal assistant, instruct this person when to accept calls and when to allow interruptions. After establishing procedures for the office, write the priorities for other daily activities in which you will be involved – personal fitness, recreation program, spiritual life, family, social life, reading, writing, personal goals, personal matters, continuing education, meditation, relaxation periods – anything you desire to accomplish on a daily plan.

Now write the amount of time you need to sleep. A friend once told me that the verse in Proverbs 20:13 is interpreted, "If you love sleep, you will end in poverty." Stay awake, work hard and smart, and you won't go hungry. Many great people in history had one thing in common: they were early risers.

In the next chart, "My Ideal Time Plan," fill in the blanks for your perfect day. Then work for that perfection.

MY IDEAL TIME PLAN

Date: _____

6:00 a.m. _____	3:00 p.m. _____
6:30 a.m. _____	3:30 p.m. _____
7:00 a.m. _____	4:00 p.m. _____
7:30 a.m. _____	4:30 p.m. _____
8:00 a.m. _____	5:00 p.m. _____
8:30 a.m. _____	5:30 p.m. _____
9:00 a.m. _____	6:00 p.m. _____
8:30 a.m. _____	6:30 p.m. _____
10:00 a.m. _____	7:00 p.m. _____
10:30 a.m. _____	7:30 p.m. _____
11:00 a.m. _____	8:00 p.m. _____
11:30 a.m. _____	8:30 p.m. _____
12:00 p.m. _____	9:00 p.m. _____
12:30 p.m. _____	9:30 p.m. _____
1:00 p.m. _____	10:00 p.m. _____
1:30 p.m. _____	10:30 p.m. _____
2:00 p.m. _____	11:00 p.m. _____
2:30 p.m. _____	11:30 p.m. _____

12:00 midnight — lights out — the human computer takes over.

Prepare each day and you will become highly organized and very effective in your work and personal life. Always allow for surprises. They are bound to occur, so be flexible and learn to adjust.

Back in my coaching days, during one game a player came off the field shaking his head and said, "They are doing this and doing this and...." I interrupted and simply told the player, "Son, just adjust." That statement stuck with me from then on. When something happened that I was not prepared for, I thought about my response to my player. I began adjusting. It actually works!

By writing out your daily plan, you will be able to make adjustments and get back on schedule. Plan. Then relax. You will accomplish three times as much as you did previously. The greatest asset of this type of plan is promoting living by action – which requires less effort than living by reaction. It is amazing how effectively a written time plan organizes our minds and our work, allowing us to become truly positive, successful individuals.

Once you develop the habit of daily planning, work out your weekly plans. Planning in advance increases your effectiveness and decreases the amount of time necessary to spend on the daily plan. After mastery of the weekly plan, develop a monthly plan, then yearly or seasonal or other plans appropriate for your work. Eventually you will have planned your future success.

I strongly encourage you to give yourself the "Test of Time." Use this time study exercise to find out how you are spending time. Then plan how to best keep your time under your control. If you don't plan for distributing your own time, others will do that for you. If you have wasted time in the past through lack of organization, that can't be helped. There is no way to change what has been done. Nevertheless, tomorrow can be different. It isn't here yet, so you can plan the entire day. Remember – time is speeding away. Don't delay. The journey will be worth your life—a life of true happiness and positive success. This truth is motivation. Your goals can be accomplished, day by day.

NOTE

In the first three lessons, I described the magic of the human computer, how it came about, and a time plan to allow you to embark upon the adventure of becoming a positive, successful leader. Before we delve into the goals program in Lesson Eight that actually maps the way to accomplishing whatever it is we want to become, we need to explore the total person-total success concept. The total person program is divided into four components:

- Building a spiritual, positive self-image.
- Seeking optimum health.
- Achieving career success.
- Reaching financial independence.

Fasten your seat belts – we are ready to enter the most important dialogue of our future lives.

LESSON FOUR

BUILDING A SPIRITUAL, POSITIVE SELF-IMAGE

SPIRITUALITY

Believing, accepting, and practicing the Attitude Technique philosophy will lead you to a plateau of success in your chosen career and throughout your lifetime. We start the action by building a positive self-image.

Your self-image controls how you feel about yourself, and it relates to how you perceive that others feel about you. By building a strong inner awareness, you will become self-confident, self-disciplined, and possess a powerful spiritual faith. In fact, a strong belief in God, permeating our lives, is the master key to the positive life we are seeking through the Attitude Technique philosophy.

It's clear to me that without a proper spiritual base we cannot become successful, positive leaders. "What profit is there if you gain the whole world and lose eternal life?" is one way of putting this. The only way we can be wise, successful, and happy is to begin with reverence for God. Our growth in wisdom comes from obeying divine laws. From the religious teachings I follow, I have come to believe that God intended for each of us to mature, excel, and live a vibrant life. This means being healthy, having the things we need to sustain our families and selves, and having careers we enjoy and a way to contribute to mankind. By putting God first in our lives, we can utilize our full potential and possess a strong positive inner self-image.

Millions of the most intelligent, learned, and scientific minds of today believe in God, strong faith, and prayer. Prayer is a spiritual exercise whereby we draw ourselves to God until we are part of God's plan and purpose. Understanding this will develop true happiness, which is the object of success. It will lead us to an enriching family and social life. It will nurture our ability to achieve smaller goals, such as the type of home we want, where we want to live, the things we want to do for our children, the friends with whom we want to associate, and many more.

Possessing a strong, positive self-image begins with true faith. Our families are the most important parts of our lives, and family is the single most important part of blending our spiritual faith into our everyday lives. This love is so strong that nothing should override its importance in our lives.

Following in the footsteps of our personal faith and family are our friendships. Having close friends and being a friendly person can add significantly to one's overall life success. People who are difficult to get along with and who deliberately avoid being decent to others will, at some point, phase themselves out of goal-oriented environments. More significantly, that type of person misses out on the happiness that can be achieved by anyone simply willing to make the effort. People may forget what you do, but they will never forget how you make them feel! An exceptional book on friendship to read is Stephen E. Ambrose's book, *Comrades*.

Along with needing a strong faith to develop a positive self-image, one also should possess patience. I really do not like using the word patience. Instead, I favor the phrase "relaxed persistence." Nevertheless, we all must develop patience, and this is another important key. Patience is a vital factor in reaching success.

Anything is possible if a person has enough faith and patience. You have probably heard the story of the man who said, "I am hungry enough to eat an elephant." Someone challenged him by saying, "How could you possibly eat an elephant?" The man replied confidently, "One bite at a time." There is almost no problem that patience cannot solve. You are never defeated until you lose your patience. When the situation looks hopeless, keep hoping. When everything looks impossible, refuse to accept defeat. Most people who succeed in the face of seemingly impossible conditions are people who simply don't know how to quit.

Great people are just ordinary people with an extraordinary amount of determination. No person will ever truly know that they have succeeded until they experience an apparent failure. The pole-vaulter cannot be certain of jumping as high as possible until he or she knocks the bar down. Reach as high as you possibly can.

Life is ten percent what happens to you and ninety percent how you react. Positive thinking people never quit. They simply adjust to a proper spiritual life, which is the foundation of the total person. A total person striving toward total success in all areas of his or her life is a free individual. That person has literally found God and no longer has a vacuum in his or her life. They follow God's command.

How did I find God? Here's my personal story:

~

I had an advantage while growing up. I lived in a loving Christian home. My father, Dr. Samuel Rice, a minister and district superintendent in the Kentucky Conference of the Methodist Church; my mother; and my older brother,

Robert Cecil, surrounded me with love and understanding. This was a proper and natural setting in which to find God.

My father gave me the right to choose my own life. Due to the influence of that Christian home, going to Sunday school and church became a pattern and then a habit in my life. I was careful of my behavior. Listening to sermon after sermon, it became automatic for me to do these things. But something was lacking. I wasn't sure just what, but there was a void in my life.

While in high school, I became captain of the football team and was named All-State quarterback. I was also a leader in student government. My plans included college, but World War II came along. I joined the Navy and was soon out to sea in the Pacific.

When we traveled over the ocean at night, all lights had to be off aboard ship. Often I went to the top deck to get some fresh air. One evening I found myself there all alone. I stood, with a light rain falling and a breeze blowing across the deck. I remember looking up into the sky and feeling that something was trying to reach me. This was my first interaction with our Father in Heaven. There were no sirens, no actual voice speaking, no special lighting effects – just a feeling and a realization that the Father was there. I sensed that I must follow Him. It wasn't strong or overwhelming, but more instinctual – that He was there and that I needed Him.

After the war, I finally went to college. Again I became captain of the football team and earned All-American honors as a quarterback. I pursued studies in social science, physical education, education, administration, and psychology. My ambition was to become a football coach and a leader. I did not really know why I wanted that life, but I thought and dreamed about it. A strong desire to do well filled me.

After marrying my beautiful wife, Phyllis, we began my coaching career. Starting in small high schools, I worked my way back to Highlands, my own high school in Fort Thomas, KY. I gained success as a coach, but my life was still incomplete.

Some time later, I was writing a book on technical football training while my family and I were on vacation. I returned home early, leaving my family to enjoy Florida for a couple of weeks longer while I spent time in isolation working on the book. Late one evening, while sitting in the living room going over some notes, I experienced the same feeling I had had years before aboard my ship at sea. I walked out on the front porch and felt a light mist and breeze. Again, I looked up into the heavens and again the Father was talking to me. I did not hear a voice. There were no bright lights or visions. There was just a feeling that He was talking to me. It became clear what I must do with my life. Somehow He had brought me into the coaching field. Now He was telling me to persevere and to devote my life to young people. From that point on, my life and my family gained a greater meaning. I had a direction. I had found God, and He was directing my life.

Many times I strayed, and doubts came; however, I only had to remember those two nights, and I was straight again – looking up, following Him. I knew that by believing in Him and depending on Him, I could do what He wanted me to do.

I sensed a positive life. He led me to realize that it was His will for me to be a very positive person and a successful individual. It was also clear that He wanted me to provide leadership.

Thinking, planning, and working took me from the

high school level into the college ranks as an assistant, as a head coach, as a director of athletics at major institutions, and eventually into the National Football League as a head football coach.

After twenty-seven years in the coaching profession, I received an invitation to become an executive in professional football. A few months later, Georgia Tech offered me a position in Atlanta as an assistant to the president and director over sports programs involving all the young people at that institution. It was a difficult decision. The financial rewards are much higher on the professional level. I had to weigh that against the opportunity to return to a position where I would be working with young people.

I kept remembering that evening when I sensed that the Heavenly Father wanted me to be involved with young people. I then realized that I couldn't decide this – that He would decide it for me.

I was tired on the night a few months later when the decision was due. Tension and pressure made me fitful, but I eventually fell asleep. The next morning, bright and early, I awakened refreshed, happy and excited because I knew what I needed to do. I was to go to Georgia Tech. Even today, I continue having a strong positive feeling that God sees me in this line of work.

In finding God, I was able to see that I have only one path: to follow Him and to accomplish the best that is in me. I have learned that God is the source of supply for all my needs. When I ask, I receive. When I seek, I find. When I knock, the door is opened to me. I believe in God, His Son, and the Holy Spirit. By allowing the Spirit to permeate my thoughts, my prayers, my work, and my very being every day, I am able to believe in myself, in my positive worth, and in my future.

~

As you strive to nurture a positive self-image, you will develop many good qualities. First of all, you will allow the human computer to assist in forming these qualities. As you move on toward the top step of this program, the human computer will begin reacting positively to any and every situation without your making any demands. This will require deep thinking.

Most importantly, you will become a giver. My father once told me, "Never judge anyone – that will be handled by the Supreme Being – but you will be able to recognize the grabbers from the givers." The giver gives time, service, talents, and possessions to God's plan. Only a giver can become a total person. Winston Churchill once said, "We make a living by what we get, but we make a life by what we give."

You may want to balance your life around a wheel of life with six spokes: God, Golden Rule, Family, Self, Job, and Country.

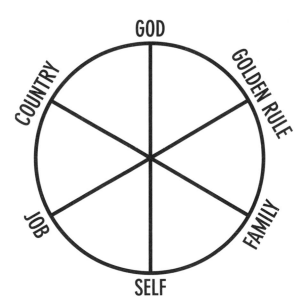

It is absolutely essential to blend a spiritual base into your life's plan. As an adjunct professor at Georgia Tech, I teach "Leadership Fitness" through the School of Applied Physiology of the College of Sciences. Primarily seniors sign up for my class each fall.

I teach many of the principles contained in this book. Georgia Tech is a state-supported institution, which requires the separation of church and state. I understand and accept this policy. Nevertheless, it is not possible to hide the spiritual component necessary for success. As a model to others in learning the relevance of spiritual faith to leadership success, I have explained how I personally believe. In class exit interviews, students occasionally ask me about my faith. Some are already strong believers in their own personal faiths; others ask for resources for their personal journeys. They want to know more about finding God and belief. A few years back, I read the book *The Case for Christ* by Lee Strobel. This manuscript is one example of how a person can go from being an atheist to a believer in a faith.

Strobel had been legal editor of the *Chicago Times* and considered himself an atheist. He decided to turn his investigative skills toward learning about Christianity in the same way that he had written about numerous criminal trials. Through that journey, he found a truth for his life and became a Christian. His book is an excellent example for both believers and doubters, and his findings will undoubtedly convince anyone of the power of true faith of God.

One of the highlights of my class is the range of outside speakers I bring to talk to students. These inspired people believe in the Attitude Technique approach to a successful life. The first speaker each year is my dear friend Bishop Bevel Jones.

I have asked Bishop Jones to contribute to *Leadership Fitness*: Bishop Jones, the Bishop in Residence at his alma mater,

The Candler School of Theology at Emory University, served several United Methodist churches over a period of thirty-five years. A teacher, author, and great friend to many outstanding people in the field of athletics, he is always a big hit with my class because of his approach to building a strong, spiritual self-image. His article to follow tells the story:

BUILDING A STRONG SELF-IMAGE

It is a privilege to have a part in this book. Homer is a great leader and a dear friend. He personifies all that he says in these pages and leads by example. I especially appreciate his sharing his own faith journey in this lesson, and I know how deep and genuine his spiritual life is. His relationship to God is the centerpiece of his character.

In the popular movie "City Slickers," Jack Palance exclaims, "Life is about one thing!" When Billy Crystal asks him what that thing is, he responds: "That's what you've got to figure out." How true that is for all of us. One of the marks of leadership is focus, a master motive. If we are to have a strong sense of our own identity, we need to be keenly aware of our Creator—the very source. St. Augustine realized after years of floundering that God has made us for Godself, and our hearts are restless until they find rest in Him. The key to Homer Rice's philosophy of the total person—and to his own life—is seeking and doing God's will.

In my late teens I came across a regimen for abundant and effective living. It consists of three principles that stand together like a three-legged stool. The first is *A Self Fit to Live With*. Fit to live with one's own self, and others also. We can be our own worst enemy. If we are at odds with ourselves, we will be at odds with other people. A positive self-image begins with oneself—attitude, spirit, self-acceptance, self-respect, self-discipline, and continual growth. The Psalmist's prayer fits all sizes: "Create in me a clean heart, O God, and renew a right spirit within me. Let the words of my mouth and the meditations of my heart be acceptable in your sight, my Strength and my Redeemer." (Psalm 51: 10).

Second, *A Purpose Fit to Live For.* A young boy missed a couple of days in school because of illness. His mother gave him a note for the teacher and told him it was his excuse for being absent. Not many days later the teacher asked her pupils to bring copies of their birth certificates for the school's records. The young lad went home and said, "Now they want my excuse for being born!" What's mine, and what's yours?

Mission is a word we customarily associate with church. Nowadays many individuals are writing personal mission statements. Corporations and institutions are doing the same. It's important to write, be specific, and keep always in mind what our purpose is and why we are doing what we do. If we are not thoughtful and careful, our actions become routine, and life is more like a treadmill than a worthwhile venture.

One of the finest men I know tells of his young adult years when he was raking in the money and thriving in his business. One day while driving home by himself from his lovely summer home on the river, the question arose like a specter in his mind: *Where are you going?* He couldn't answer that. He stopped his car on the shoulder of the highway and grappled with that issue. It marked a turning point in his life, a reorganizing of his priorities, concern more for persons than for material gain, and a primary regard for the things of God. He has moved from mere success to significance. Once he was filled full. Now he is fulfilled. The purpose has made all the difference.

Third, *A Faith Fit to Live By.* Without faith, life has no solid foundation. H.G. Wells, the historian, said that until we find

God and are found by God, we begin at no beginning and we work to no end. Scripture says that faith is the substance of things hoped for and the evidence of things not seen (Hebrews 11:1) Faith is not fanciful, having to do with fairy tales and make-believe. It is not trying to believe something you know isn't true. Faith is believing what you cannot prove but can't help believing. It doesn't go against reason, but beyond reason. Call it reason grown courageous. Better still, it is betting your life there is a God, a good and great God – one who is faithful and loving and will never let you down.

Faith corresponds with hope. I saw a bumper sticker the other day that said, "I sure do feel better now that I've given up hope." The truth is that where there's hope, there's life. We are not talking about optimism, but hardheaded hope: not wishing, but trusting. Martin Luther, the great reformer, said, "Faith is a living, daring confidence in God's grace, so sure and certain that the believer would stake his life on it a thousand times."

If we are to be strong, positive, and steadfast, we need hope born of faith. This means never giving up. Not that we are convinced everything will turn out well but because we are confident what we are doing is right regardless of how it turns out!

Recently I came upon a statement that strengthened my spirit and no doubt will yours:

> *Faith is hearing tomorrow's music.*
> *Hope is dancing to it today!*

Keep dancing.

L. BEVEL JONES
United Methodist Bishop, retired

Bevel Jones teaches us that having faith always gives us hope. Without hope, we are defeated and never win. As believers, we have extreme hope. Without hope, we do not expect anything. Faith and hope set us free to think thoughts that lead us to life-enriching opportunities. With relaxed perseverance, we should persist in making full use of the ideas that flow into our human computer, in making the right choices, and in beginning action upon those decisions. Altering the word *patience* to *relaxed persistence* clearly fits our new life. We become free to believe, and gain faith that we have been created for life as part of a magnificent design of life and renewal. The story of Gen. James Dozier's faith and communication with God is a great example to remember.

In December 1981, the Red Brigade terrorist group kidnapped the deputy chief of staff for the North Atlantic Treaty Organization's Southern Region in Verona, Italy. Brigadier General James L. Dozier was kept chained and in captivity for forty-two days. During his ordeal he stayed in constant communication with God. He believed God would guide him and that the whole affair would work out for good ends. He believed others, including his wife Judy, his family, and his friends, were praying for him. Despite his situation, he visualized his release, the press conference, and the welcome by the authorities and his friends. He kept these positive thoughts throughout the time he was held. That visualization became a reality when a crack anti-terrorist unit freed him. His impressions, sustained in captivity, worked out in reality, producing the press conference and a welcome home, just as he had pictured them.

Your self-faith will lead to an experience of joy and fulfillment. As John Wesley said, "Teach faith until you have it yourself." I feel this way as I teach my class "Leadership Fitness" and speak about the human computer to students as well as other various groups. Faith is a powerful self-tool.

In sports, we hear and read a lot about the negatives. But one organization that is a positive influence is the Fellowship of Christian Athletes (FCA). My good friend Dal Shealy, a former successful collegiate football coach and now President of FCA, developed a program called "The Competitor's Creed" that embodies how this organization puts its faith into practice. He explains the purpose and details of "The Competitor's Creed" in Appendix C. That program helps to instill a commitment in coaches and athletes to provide positive leadership and to be role models. The result: it works!

God allows us to become whatever we decide to be. He allows us to live as we choose. Therefore, each individual is the sum of his or her thoughts. The human computer can aid you in building a positive self-image. Always remember that we are sustained by a higher power, regardless of our situation. It's simple to decide to be a self-confident human being who will succeed positively. Start now to become the person you should be and want to become. You will lead others to the winner's circle.

Taking one day at a time is an important step to living a life of health, peace, and fulfillment. We can alleviate regret about the past and fear about the future when we trust in God to guide us daily and we follow through with the right action.

We can plan for the future, but we do so only by living productively in the time we call today. Each prayer we pray, each divine idea we implement in our daily living, and each positive step we take today prepares us for tomorrow.

If thinking about an entire day of activity or inactivity causes you feelings of anxiety, then take one hour at a time, or even one moment at a time. We may need to affirm our faith, our strength, and our health in order to build on the truth of our affirmations. We are whole and complete in God, and today is a day of accomplishment and fulfillment. "This is a day which the Lord has made; let us rejoice and be glad in it." (Psalms 118:24)

Don Harp, the popular minister of Peachtree Road United Methodist Church in Atlanta, recently made the following remarks about leadership in a sermon to his congregation. Don, a dear friend and our minister, is a successful, positive leader in the realm of spirituality.

He said that in becoming a good leader, it is most important to set a good moral example. A simple and time-tested guide for moral leadership would be the Ten Commandments. In our halls of Congress, most of our laws are based on these true and simple laws.

One easy-to-remember formula is,

1. Live by principles instead of feelings.

2. Associate with people of integrity. They will be great examples to you.

3. Reject anything that tempts you to lower your standards.

In every arena of life, we all look up to those who set good moral examples. If you are striving to be a good leader, a fundamental quality to attain will be that of being a good moral leader.

As my wife, Phyllis, and I have found in our own involvement in this church, one of the most rewarding aspects of taking part in a religious community is the exposure it gives to positive leaders, especially through the Timothy Sunday School Class in which we participate.

But wherever you live or worship, you'll find positive leaders. Seek them out and learn from them.

LESSON FIVE

OPTIMUM HEALTH

In your efforts to become a positive, successful leader, you must strive for optimum health. If you don't feel well or if you have an unhealthy lifestyle, you will not be at your best. A positive leader must be fit for the job at many levels. This requires a medical and fitness check-up periodically to keep score on your health. Many elements make up a top physically fit leader.

- A planned fitness program
- Planned recreation
- Proper rest
- Relaxation techniques
- Proper nutrition
- Mental stimulation
- Solitude
- Laughter (humor)

One can survive a major illness if body, mind, and faith work in concert to lessen the chance of a bad outcome.

As a seventeen-year old high school senior and football player, I was in peak physical and mental condition. The time was 1944, when the United States was in the middle of World War II. I soon left for the Navy, and after basic training (boot camp), I was assigned to a ship bound for the South Pacific and eventually for a base in the Philippine Islands. At the time, the United States military was planning an attack – an unprecedented naval and aerial bombardment – on Kyushu, the southernmost of the Japanese home islands.

Fortunately, the war ended in August 1945, and I was reassigned for duty in the occupation of Japan. But before our ship sailed, I came down with an attack of malaria. Several of my shipmates died of that terrible disease, but I survived. My good fitness, condition, faith, and strong mental attitude helped me to overcome the disease. I knew I had to survive in order to fulfill my mission and purpose to return home, attend college, compete in collegiate athletics, and become a coach to prepare young men for successful careers. My mental state pulled me through that difficult period of my life.

Eventually I completed my plan to enter the coaching/teaching field. However, as years passed, even though I was involved in training football teams for competitive action, I somehow let my fitness program disappear. I paid very little attention to my personal health. Believing I could outwork my opponents, I slept only a few hours at night and became a workaholic. While undergoing a medical exam for a life insurance policy, my blood pressure went off the board. I could no longer ignore my unhealthy lifestyle.

During this period, I met the famous cardiologist Dr. Kenneth Cooper at a seminar where we were both scheduled to speak. His motivational speech about health fitness and preventive medicine probably saved my life. He gave me one of his early books, which I read cover to cover in one sitting. Dr. Cooper's advice convinced me at age thirty-eight that I had to begin a rigorous fitness program. Nutrition had to be a priority, and I needed to sleep at least six hours at night. I continued this program for many years.

In time, I had to face another dreaded disease when cancer struck my body. I underwent surgery for prostate cancer, then later for kidney cancer. In each case, the physician told me that my fitness and good health had pulled me through. As a two-time cancer survivor, I again had beaten the odds. As of this writing at age seventy-seven, I am in excellent health and continue the point program for good health.

PLANNED FITNESS PROGRAM

Dr. Kenneth Cooper developed the Aerobics Fitness Program. I am a strong advocate of his preventative approach. His work attacks the problem of disorders of the cardiovascular system, lungs, and nervous system through planned activities that include running, walking, cycling, swimming, and tennis, among other forms of exercise.

Dr. Cooper came up with the aerobic point score as part of a systematic program for our physical benefit. An aerobic program will improve the quality of one's life. Research proves that we can prevent illness by participating in this type of program. I heartily recommend Dr. Cooper's books about these issues.

PLANNED RECREATION

A health/fitness program must also include planned recreation. This can be tennis, golf, fishing, boating, or whatever activity you desire. The specific activity can include your family, thus serving two vital purposes.

PROPER REST

Proper rest is essential. Each person must find the number of hours needed for proper rest. Do not oversleep, however, because that can dull your senses and hold back opportunities. During the most productive years of my career, I managed to sleep six hours each night. Some health experts recommend seven to eight hours per night.

Whatever you can manage and still feel well rested the next morning is sufficient. Some of our great leaders have managed on a short nap of ten to twenty minutes several times a day. I believe that the objective is to achieve as much as you can during your hours awake. If you are dull and tired, you may make costly mistakes. A well-planned day is the key.

RELAXATION TECHNIQUES

Relaxation is also necessary for good health and productivity. Take one or two periods each day, of fifteen to twenty minutes each, to relax completely. This can be a time for meditation. Go to a darkened room where you will not be disturbed. Relax every part of your body. Do not think of anything. You might even drop off to sleep for a few minutes, and that can be your nap for the day. Start with your toes, working up to each part of your body and visualizing each part completely relaxed. Relax your hips, shoulders, and facial muscles. Experience quietness.

Relaxation also means taking a full, planned vacation.

PROPER NUTRITION

Proper nutrition is essential to a vibrant life. Work out a nutritional program that fits your body's mechanism. Dr. Chris Rosenbloom, Associate Professor of Nutrition at Georgia State University, is an authority on the subject. She offers extended nutrition advice in Appendix D.

A healthy, nutritional lifestyle must include a study of the vitamin-mineral story. Dr. Alexander Bralley, the founder of Metametrix Clinical Laboratory, has developed a program that should be seriously considered for a healthy life, preventing serious illnesses, and, in some cases, slowing down the aging process. The Case for Supplements is explained in Appendix E.

MENTAL STIMULATION

Mental stimulation is just as much a part of our well-being as any area of health. By studying and reading challenging books, we exercise the brain with deep thinking. Set aside a short time each day for reading to increase your mental capacity. You must have knowledge to achieve a successful life, and reading is the best way to acquire it. Some of our top leaders have exciting hobbies that keep them intellectually sharp and growing stronger mentally. One of my hobbies happens to be reading and studying American history. One part of our history that captures my interest is the Lewis and Clark expedition of 1804-1806.

SOLITUDE
(OR, THE LEWIS AND CLARK EXPEDITION)

In the early 1980s, I met William (Bill) E. Moore, a Georgia Tech graduate from 1938. Bill had been captain of the tennis team and became a highly successful entrepreneur. He expressed interest in helping me with my student/athlete total person program. His contributions were a tremendous aid for my work in exposing young people to "Leadership Fitness." With Bill and another close friend, Albert "Bud" Parker (also a tennis great from Georgia Tech), we formed a fishing trio. In the winter we traveled to my home in Marco Island for gulf fishing, and during the summer we visited Bill's Broken O Ranch in Montana for fly-fishing. We were serious fishermen and spent much time in the Sun River that flows through Bill's property. During our visits to the ranch, Bill introduced me to the journals of the famous Lewis and Clark Expedition. I became fascinated with that part of our American history. In time, I read many books on the subject, particularly Stephen E. Ambrose's *Undaunted Courage*.

In 1803, President Thomas Jefferson selected Captain Meriwether Lewis to lead an expedition to locate a water route across the continent to the Pacific Ocean. Lewis asked his friend, Captain William Clark, to join him on this trip. Their small party moved up the Missouri River to the Rockies but failed to find the much-desired water pathway.

They had to climb over the Rockies to eventually discover the Columbia River that led them to their destination. This journey through the new Louisiana Purchase territory opened up the west. On their return trip, Lewis and some of his men camped on the Sun River where Bill Moore's Ranch is located today. In a way, the Lewis and Clark journey became a hobby that led me to perfect solitude. Bill eventually set up quarters on the ranch so I could go out anytime and fish. I accepted this kind offer and began fly fishing the Sun River.

To be alone, wading the river, moving into position for a rainbow or brown trout to strike is *solitude* at the highest level. The water is cool and refreshing, the sky is big and blue, the Rockies in the distance display their snowcaps, an eagle flies overhead, perhaps a deer or antelope will run by on the bank, and there you are in a game with a trout. You land a rainbow, bring him in, kneel down, and he is released back to the stream. If I had problems in the real world to resolve, I forgot what they were when I was on that river. I thank God for this wonderful world He has created and that I am part of it. This is solitude, and it is an important ingredient to mix in with your health/fitness program. Time alone, away from the office and people, and, of course, away from negatives – that's one important step toward optimum health.

Successful people find solitude in many different ways. It might be a certain hobby, a trip to the lake or beach, or some other solitary activity. Solitude should be a planned part of your daily schedule. Without it we can be controlled by elements detrimental to our health, both mentally and physically. Solitude is powerful. It can erase stress and promote good health.

LAUGHTER

The final step to optimum health is laughter and good humor. Laughing can be a wonderful therapy. It will strengthen the body and pick up your spirits. When we laugh, invigorating agents called endorphins are released into our bodies. We become energized as the cells of our bodies are recharged through happiness. Laughter may be the hidden secret to good health. When we laugh – truly laugh, not with a forced outburst – we feel good, happy, and free of negative thoughts. Laughter is a positive reaction.

Even medical researchers are taking laughter seriously as a healer for illnesses. There are claims that a sense of humor has saved lives. Without humor, we live dull and unhappy lives. My friend Bud Parker consistently sends me humorous cartoons. He doesn't realize how many times his mailings have changed my negative thoughts to positive ones.

A good laugh gets the heart beating faster, brings in extra oxygen, and stimulates blood circulation. We feel better, our whole body relaxes, and disease-fighting immune cells go into production. Remember Norman Cousins' *Anatomy of an Illness*? He believed that laughter – along with hope, faith, the will to live, purpose, and determination – can assist medical science in its struggle against life-threatening diseases.

In the 1950s and 1960s, my wife Phyllis and our three young daughters (Nancy, Phyllis, and Angie) traveled with me each summer to the Fellowship of Christian Athletes Conference. The spiritually uplifting conference featured a minister, Grady Knutt, who was undoubtedly the funniest man in America. I would literally roll in the aisle. We all felt blessed and, indeed, healthy from his performance. Grady later joined the cast of the TV show "Hee-Haw."

I asked my good friend and cardiologist, Dr. John D. Cantwell – chief medical officer of the 1996 Olympic Games in Atlanta, medical director of the Homer Rice Center for Sports Performance at Georgia Tech, frequent speaker to the Leadership Fitness class, and also physician for the Atlanta Braves – to contribute a program of good health and fitness to *Leadership Fitness*. He shares his knowledge about "How to Be a Survivor: Guidelines on Living Well to Age 100" in Appendix F.

Following the plan presented in this lesson has kept me going with a high energy level. It is critically important to be physically, mentally, and spiritually fit in order to lead others to the top step and to be a positive successful leader.

Football coach.

With Georgia Tech Athletic Director Dave Braine in front of Homer's plaque
on Tech's Wall of Legends.

How could I turn down Rice University when they named the stadium "Rice Stadium?"

As an athlete!

Author of 7 major books as adjunct professor at Georgia Tech.

Director of Athletics at the University of North Carolina, with wife Phyllis
and daughters (l to r) Angie, Phyllis and Nancy.

A victory interview after Homer Rice's Cincinnati Bengals defeated the World Champion
Pittsburg Steelers 34 to 10 in 1979.

Retirement as Georgia Tech's Director of Athletics and Executive Assistant to the President.

With Phyllis in front of The Homer Rice Center.

Phyllis Rice, the head coach in the Rice family.

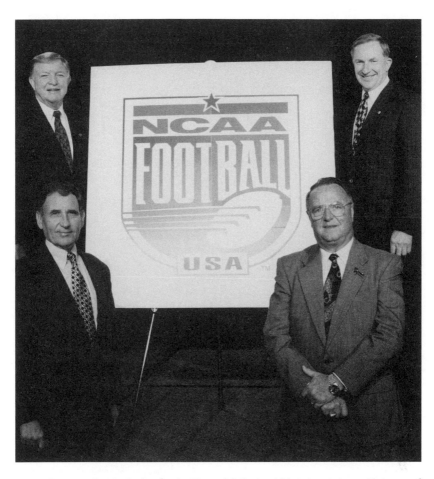

Homer Rice providing leadership for the National Collegiate Athletic Association as Chairman of the NCAA's Football Rules Comittee.

Homer Rice (bottom left); Grant Teaff, Executive Director of the American Football Coaches Association (top left); Cedric Demsey, Executive Director of the NCAA (top right); Bobby Bowen, Head Football Coach at Florida State (bottom right).

LESSON SIX

ACHIEVING CAREER SUCCESS
THROUGH SELF-CONTROLLED MOTIVATION

SELF MOTIVATION—CONTROLLED VISUALIZATION

The external world is intertwined with the inner world. Each is inseparable from the whole. A person's psychological state affects his or her day-to-day life and health, and likewise, a person's day-to-day life affects his or her psychological health. We now turn to a technique for organizing one's life to become a total person – a whole person – positioned for total success. That technique is the art of controlled visualization.

CAREER SUCCESS
THROUGH SELF-CONTROLLED MOTIVATION

The key to a successful career is self-motivation. After we master this key, we can begin teaching staff/employees or whatever group we lead the art of self-motivation. I take the concept a step higher and call it self-written motivation. By writing your thoughts on paper, you will seal them in your human computer and call upon them when needed. Everything begins with an idea. If we can control our minds, we can control our future and our career success.

To become completely successful we must base everything on truth. If we are not truthful, we will fail. A lie cannot withstand the test of time. Truthful motivation is a spark that ignites us to do great things. We plan it. We write it. We may even record it on tape. We begin acting out the role we must play to accomplish our goals. Consistency and repetition pay off. The role becomes a ladder to climb. The higher we climb, the more aware we become of our potential.

Self-motivation, or self-written motivation, involves seven principles. Each principle represents a step up the ladder.

THE FIRST PRINCIPLE IS HAVING
THE DESIRE TO ACCOMPLISH SOMETHING

Whatever it is, you must fix it in your mind in exact detail. Write it so it will become absolutely clear. This is the commitment and the beginning. Once you make the decision in writing, you then set a target date, giving yourself a deadline to work toward. Without a finishing point, you will never complete your desire. Once you establish a target date, you begin to write the ingredients necessary to achieve your goal. You may want to take it one step further and write a *plan of action* for gaining your desire. The next step is very important: You must declare what you're willing to give. Whatever your goal, you will never receive anything without first giving. It may be something as simple as your time or your effort, but you must give before you expect to receive.

After writing your desire or need, the target date, the ingredients and a plan of action, and what you are willing to give, you should begin to visualize your desire as already completed. Visualization is the beginning of the climb upward. The more you visualize the finished product, the closer you will move toward its realization. By reading your written statements each day, you bring that desire into focus. Then you must strive for its completion. The power of visualization will manage your life toward completing what you desire.

Desire is a prime motivating force in all of us. There are comparatively few people with great desire. Most are content to go along occupying the tiny niches in which they find themselves. They accept their positions in life as something that fate has fixed for them, and very seldom do they make either a mental or physical effort to extract themselves from those positions. Successful people realize that the greatest power is produced by desire. Whatever we fix our thoughts upon is the thing that we attract to us.

When you start, you may have no idea what the results will be. Don't concern yourself with this; leave it to the human computer. You will find that you receive assistance from the most unexpected sources. When you get an idea, follow it. Keep a note pad handy. When ideas come, even during the night, write them on the pad so they will not be lost. This is very important.

Edison kept a notebook, and his best ideas for many of his inventions came while he slept. Early in my career, as a young high school football coach, I awakened at 2:00 a.m. and diagrammed an offensive play on a pad by my nightstand. Little did I realize that this idea would become the triple option, one of the greatest innovations in the history of football. The person with a fixed thought, a clear picture of the desire, or an idea always before him causes it, through repetition, to be buried deep in his or her subconscious. That person is thus enabled, thanks to the brain's generative and sustaining power, to realize the goal in a minimum of time and physical effort. Pursue your thoughts unceasingly. Step by step, you will achieve your goal because all of your faculties and powers are directed toward that end.

Two objects cannot occupy the same space at the same time. Compare your mind to that space: it can't be filled with negative thoughts or doubts if you have it filled with positive, powerful, and creative thoughts. Whatever your desire may be, do not limit your thinking to a small area. Encompass broader fields of experience and action. Most people limit themselves to habits of thought that include their small, everyday happenings. Those patterns become chains that bind them to lives of inactivity, poverty, and limitation. Learn to think big. Your brain cells are aching for exercise in large visions. Everyone knows how to think small. It takes a truly expanded mind to think big.

How do you develop a desire, an idea? *Think*. Think inspired thoughts. Think creatively and dynamically. Think big. Think successful thoughts. Think wholesome thoughts. Think healthy thoughts. Visualize great things. Visualize achievement, perfection, and the situation you wish to be in. *Feel*. Feel your thoughts. Feel healthy and strong. Feel wholesome and successful, confident and poised. *Act*. Act with confidence, decisiveness. Be aggressive and have positive boldness in your actions. Play the part you wish to fill on the stage of life. Make your own decisions as to what you want to be, but set into motion the law of action by taking the first step.

Positive, creative thoughts, desires, or ideas lead to action and ultimately to their realization. The real power, much more than the action itself, is the thought. Whatever a person can conceive mentally, he or she can bring into effect. Desire is the first principle in self-motivation.

THE SECOND PRINCIPLE IS BELIEF

We must have a strong belief in the outcome. This is a state of mind that may be created by affirmation or repeated instructions to the human computer – the subconscious mind. Be persistent about attaining your desire. A mental image of yourself already accomplishing what you want, seen over and over again, will project the belief you need to achieve your goals.

Belief is related to faith. Our faith in God aids us in finding our identity with the Creator of the Universe. The world is filled with people who have worked hard but have little to show for it. Something more than hard work is necessary. That something is creative thinking and a firm belief in your ability to execute your ideas. Determine precisely what you want. You must have a mental pattern clearly drawn in your mind. Most people have a general idea that they would like to be successful, but beyond that everything is vague.

You must know precisely where you are headed. Keep a fixed desire or idea in view, and have faith, strong faith, that you will receive. Belief in yourself and in your destiny is an essential and important step in your climb up the ladder. "All things are possible to him that believes." We must work hard but we must also work smart.

THE THIRD PRINCIPLE IS IMAGINATION

A person can create anything he or she can imagine. Whatever we can visualize and believe in, we can achieve. All great people develop the power of self-motivation.

The power to create new ideas comes from combining previous experiences with vision. When you creatively imagine something, you are actually causing it to come into being. The process by which it comes to pass is a mystery, but the method for making it happen is this: Picture the things you want to do; hold them in consciousness; and pattern your actions in such a way that you are constantly working toward the fulfillment of the desires you hold in your imagination.

THE FOURTH PRINCIPLE IS ORGANIZATION OF PLANNING

Whatever you desire in life cannot be done alone. Select one or more individuals to work with you in developing your plan. The more minds you can bring together working for a common purpose, the more related information is available. As a leader, you need to take into confidence a small team or group and listen to their ideas. Great ideas are a combination of related ideas. Pick the individuals or group with care. They must be hard and smart working, conscientious people you respect. You can have a lot of fun, and you will reach your desire much sooner.

Arrange to meet with your group at least once a week. Refine your plans until they are perfected. Each day you must know exactly what you are going to do and why. You must be a positive leader to direct your plan. Planning requires concentration. It is difficult to concentrate for any length of time. Our thoughts and ideas flow through our mind with astonishing rapidity.

You are constantly being swayed by what you read, see, and hear. As a result, the coordinating part of the creative force turns to the task of gathering these scattered elements into a confused mass, instead of developing itself to make a clear and dynamic picture of your desire. This is the primary reason we must write our desires and the plans that we will follow.

The mind must be held steady to the desire. Successful minds work to a single point. When concentrating, allow nothing to interfere with your mental concentration. Pick a definite time each day and sit quietly by yourself, concentrating your mental power on what you are trying to achieve. Organized planning will take you a step closer to your desired goal. By rearranging daily work so that we can succeed in little things, we build an atmosphere of success that will carry over into larger and more important undertakings.

THE FIFTH PRINCIPLE IS TO BE ABLE TO MAKE DECISIONS

Decision-making is a necessary skill. Lack of decisiveness is the major cause of failure. Successful people reach decisions promptly and change them slowly, if there ever is a need for change. Failures reach decisions very slowly and change them rapidly. However, never make an important decision without getting all the facts. It is better to pause or hold until the facts are in and then to make a decision that is the best for the program – and stay with it. Most people are afraid to take on responsibilities, to make decisions, and to step out alone. That's why there are so few leaders and so many followers. When confronted with a problem, you will find that the longer you put it off, the greater it becomes, and the less confident you are of your ability to solve it. Learn to make decisions, because in not deciding, you fail to act; and in failing to act, you invite complete failure. All great people are people of quick decision. A quick decision ignites initiative, accumulated knowledge, and experience.

Abraham Lincoln once said, "If I were to try to react, much less answer, all the attacks on me, this shop might as well be closed for any other business. I do the very best I know how, the very best I can; and I mean to keep on doing so until the end. If the end brings me out all right, then what is said against me won't matter. If the end brings me out wrong, then ten angels swearing I was right would make no difference."

The important thing to remember is that mistakes are human. None of us can bat .1,000, but we bat zero if we never step up to home plate.

THE SIXTH PRINCIPLE: WE MUST HAVE PERSISTENCE

When everything indicates it is all over, go the extra mile and succeed. This is the difference between success and failure. This is the separation of men from boys and women from girls. Persistence is a state of mind. It can, therefore, be cultivated. Persistence is the result of the habits we form. All successful coaches are persistent. They keep coming back against great odds, and they succeed. Paul Brown, Vince Lombardi, John Wooden, Paul Bryant, Eddie Robinson, Bud Wilkinson, and many other great coaches experienced defeat but would not give in. Their imagination and will power took them to the top.

Persistence creates a winning attitude. This means that you know what you want. Believe you can get it, work with all you have to achieve it, and refuse to give up under any odds.

THE SEVENTH PRINCIPLE – AND THE ULTIMATE KEY TO POSITIVE LEADERSHIP, SUCCESS, AND TRUE HAPPINESS – IS THE UNDERSTANDING OF THE HUMAN COMPUTER, THE SUBCONSCIOUS MIND

Once you understand this personal machine and put it to positive, worthwhile, and constructive use, your life and your success can be, and will be, whatever you want it to be. In fact, there is no way it can be otherwise.

The human computer controls our minds, our thoughts, and our destinies. The scientific explanation is simple. By using the

Attitude Technique, we control our thought process with positive, worthwhile affirmations. We may not understand completely the process of the brain and the two minds – conscious and subconscious – to which it is connected, but we do understand that it is the most powerful force the world has ever known. Think of all the miraculous things this human computer has given us: supersonic aircraft, spaceships to the moon, and the unbelievable power of the computer. Yet experts tell us that we use only a small percentage of our capabilities. Our potential is unlimited. This power is available to anyone who will only take the time to utilize its greatness.

I once heard a speaker tell the story of the legend of the creation of the universe: A committee held a conference and one member said, "Let us give to man the same creative power that we ourselves possess." The committee agreed, but one asked, "Where shall we hide this priceless gift?" Another answered, "Let us hide it where man will never think to look for it – within his own mind."

From a very early age, perhaps even in your mother's womb, everything you heard, saw, or felt was stored in your subconscious (human computer). Your conscious mind collects and your subconscious stores and performs. This is the exact process of a computer. The input (what we program into the computer) is our storehouse of information. The input subsequently determines actions, or output. Your human computer does not care what you give it. It will perform with whatever material is input. If you have given it negative, unworthy thoughts all these years, then you will perform as a negative person. When you do something you are sorry for later, it cannot be helped because this is your human computer performing as you have programmed it to do.

Our human computer is constantly at work molding our thoughts, feelings and actions. This computer is our inner power. It is recognized as the essence of life, and the limits of its power are unknown. It never sleeps. It comes to our support in time of great trouble. It warns us of impending danger. Often it aids us to do something that seems impossible. When properly employed, it performs so-called miracles. Objectively, it does as it is told. That is, it performs when and as it is commanded. Subjectively, it acts primarily upon its own initiative.

When this principle is fully comprehended, the result becomes breathtaking. Every student of the subject understands what can be accomplished by controlling our planned thoughts. Many have employed it to achieve fame and worthiness for the good of mankind. Its power is available to anyone. If you believe in its power and put it to work for you, it can and will shape and control your life. It can be used to solve a problem or achieve anything desired strongly enough by the individual.

How can you use it for your benefit? First, through positive prayer, be sure that you are asking for something that is rightfully yours to have and is within your ability to handle. The human computer manifests only according to the capabilities of the person.

Many people get into situations or positions that they cannot handle. It is better to wait for your desire until you are prepared. Second, you must have patience and absolute faith. Our computer will not work unless we believe it can. Start saying, "I believe, I believe." Say it 100 times. When you verbalize "I believe," your human computer responds and begins recording. This is the power of suggestion. You are not saying, "I do not believe."

Only one thought can occupy your mind. Therefore, if you keep that positive thought – "I believe" – in your conscious mind, your human computer will accept it, and you will begin believing. This is the Attitude Technique: training yourself toward successful positive leadership. You control your thoughts; therefore, you begin controlling your performance. Your computer cannot tell the difference between negative and positive thoughts. The computer accepts whatever thought you give it.

Your need must be conveyed to the human computer as if the work has already been accomplished. Many times something happens that you feel has happened before. And often times it has, but only in your subconscious. While it is necessary for you to feel and to think yourself successful, it is important for you to go one step further and actually *see* yourself as a positive, successful leader. The final step is to wait patiently while the subconscious assimilates the elements of your problem and then goes about its own way to solve for you. The solution – the correct course of action that you must follow immediately and unquestioningly – will be revealed to you. There must be no hesitation on your part, no mental reservation, no deliberation. Take the course of action. One day you will find yourself, through the aid of the human computer, in the position you sought.

All of us have seen and experienced how, in difficult situations or sudden emergencies, our spontaneous action is always best. We have witnessed superhuman strength in individuals who were able to perform feats far beyond their normal powers. I remember watching a young basketball player only 5'8" dunk a basket to win a particular game. It was the only way he could have scored when heavily guarded under the goal by two giants on each side of him. Neither before nor since could he dunk a basketball. We have seen the 9.4 sprinter speeding toward a sure touchdown when suddenly the 10.5 defensive back comes from out of nowhere to overtake him. As one of Coach Bear Bryant's players once remarked, "He was only running for a touchdown; I was running for my life." We see it happen in the sports world often, and it's not uncommon in the outside world. An overturned automobile pins a person underneath. His friend lifts the back end of the car, enabling the victim to roll to safety. Great rescues are related to the subconscious (human computer). So are heroic acts in war. This same power can give us whatever we want in our professional leadership careers.

The human computer always brings to reality whatever it is led to believe. Human imagination and concentration are the chief factors in developing the forces of the subconscious. Once you believe in your subconscious mind, you can utilize it for various situations. If you want to awaken at a certain time in the morning without using an alarm clock, just preorder your human computer to awaken you. If you have a problem, write it and then tell your human computer to give you the answer. It will never fail.

Repetition is a fundamental process. Repeated positive thoughts and suggestions can bring you success. Many people become confused and frustrated because they allow themselves to be influenced by the negative thoughts and action of others. Repetition of negative thoughts, if continued long enough, will discourage even the most powerful. We are all victims of suggestion. Get a clear picture of what you want, and keep telling yourself that you are going to get it. Then go to work, always keeping your goal in mind.

This program is not a ticket to fame and success overnight. It is intended only as a key to unlock the door that leads to the goal of your desire. Do not allow memories of past failures to affect your present performance. If you dwell upon them — "I failed yesterday, therefore, I will fail today." – you will assure that result. The moment you change your mind and stop giving power to the past; your past mistakes will lose power over you. "If you believe you can, or if you believe you can't, you are right."

Your human computer operates in terms of goals and end results. Once you give it a definite goal to achieve, you can depend upon its guidance system to take you to that end. You supply the desire by thinking in terms of the finished product. Your human computer supplies the means. The reason is simple:

when you feel successful and self-confident, you act successfully. When the feeling is strong enough, you can literally do no wrong. In time, you will not only feel successful, but you will expect to be successful. You can train your human computer by building habits to perform any act you choose consciously. It will, in time, carry out any command that you give it.

You first must believe in its power, and then you must control your thoughts.

By constant repetition of positive thought, you will imprint it on your human computer, making it a part of the automatic reflex action of your subconscious mind. When you constantly report positive statements such as, "I am healthy, I have positive energy, I am happy," you actually raise the energy level of your body and release stored sugar in the liver, giving you greater vitality. On the other hand, negative suggestions such as, "I feel sick, I am tired, I feel terrible, I will catch cold," actually create the mental and physical atmosphere in which these negative conditions breed. When you act a part long enough, your human computer (subconscious mind) makes it a living reality.

Be certain, however, not to misuse your human computer. If it is employed for harmful or evil purposes, it will destroy you. The seven principles form an insurance policy against failure. They develop in you a sixth sense that comes from mastering the seven principles. It comes slowly by meditation, self-examination, and serious thought. The mind begins to work affirmatively and positively without any demands from the individual. It takes years of experience to develop this sense, but the minute you start your life takes on a new and different meaning. You begin to grow and mature a little each day. You become happy. Your health, your work, and your family and spiritual life improve. The change is so significant that you will wonder why you waited so long to grasp the new life. But it is never too late To go after the best.

We are the result of what we have thought. Your life is the result of your thought processes. The secret of success lies not without but within. Thought is the original source of all great things. Our thoughts make or break us. We become what we contemplate. We also are molded by the thoughts of others — by what we hear, read and see. If those thoughts are negative, we must learn to keep free of them. Our thoughts determine our conversation, our posture, and our facial expressions. Fear often tints our thoughts negatively. Fear is basically an imaginary factor. Changing from a fearful thought to a positive thought wipes out the imagination of a developed fear. The object of practicing thought and action is to make repeated trials and constantly correct errors until a hit is scored. A person is literally what he or she thinks, their character being the complete sum of their thoughts. Repeated positive thoughts and actions will develop the sixth sense.

Now that we have become self-motivated, we are prepared to teach others this power. First we must try to understand the other person. A motivated individual thinks of the work he or she does; the achievement on the job; responsibilities; advancement as a result of work accomplished; and recognition (notice, praise, or blame) in connection with work accomplished. A non-motivated individual thinks of: salary; supervision; working conditions; status; job security; staff policies, administration, and staff members. The employee or staff person who allows negative thoughts to rule the day is not focused on his or her responsibilities. That could be the fault of the leader for not building a positive attitude within the workforce. The most valuable asset in any organization is its workers. A leader must train, develop, and motivate people in a manner that wins confidence and gets results. An old adage says: "One percent make things happen, nine percent watch things happen, and ninety percent ask, 'What happened?'" The winning organization is united 100 percent to make things happen.

Our employees see their superiors as either
highly motivated or poorly motivated
This chart illustrates how those you lead see you

HOW THE WORKER SEES HIS OR HER BOSS

HIGHLY MOTIVATED	POORLY MOTIVATED
1. Easy to talk to, even under pressure	You have to pick carefully the time you talk to him
2. Tries to see the merit in your ideas, even if they conflict with his	Because he's the boss, he tends to assume his ideas are the best
3. Tries to help his people understand staff objectives	Lets people figure out for themselves how staff objectives apply to them
4. Tries to give his people all the information they want	Provides his people with as much information as he thinks they need
5. Has consistent, high expectations of staff members	His expectations of subordinates can change from day to day
6. Tries to encourage people to reach out in new directions	Tries to protect his people from taking big risks
7. Takes your mistakes in stride, so long as you learn from them	Allows little room for mistakes, especially those that might embarrass him
8. Tries mainly to correct mistakes and figure out how they can be prevented in the future	When something goes wrong, he primarily tries to find out who caused it
9. Expects superior performance and gives credit when you do it	Expects you to do an adequate job; doesn't say much unless something goes wrong

How can we aid our staff members to become motivated and to work effectively? We must give each one a challenging job, a feeling of achievement, a sense of responsibility and growth, a chance for advancement, an atmosphere of enjoyment of work, and an opportunity for earned recognition. Staff members become dissatisfied when opportunities for achievement are eliminated, and then they become insensitive to their environment.

More importantly, we motivate others by being motivated ourselves with the Positive Mental Attitude Technique. But it must be done in such a subtle way that it does not turn off others. Motivation of others requires good communication. Once you fully understand and begin applying the seven principles, you can begin teaching the principles to your group. Before you go into a competitive situation, close your eyes and say to yourself, "I'm as good as my competitor; as a matter of fact, I am better. I can win." Repeat this several times. Open your eyes and be amazed at the results.

Motivation is personal. It is not a system or formula but rather a way of life. Motivation is internal. A person can be stimulated but cannot be manipulated for long. Eventually he or she will respond only to a challenge and to quality leadership. Motivation involves change within the individual. When he or she is motivated, the person has a desire to improve, to create, and to do constructive work. We were born with motivation, but along the way we retreat or compromise with fear or weaknesses. Our creative impulses and desires to be constructive have been suppressed, restricted, or eliminated, but we can overcome fear by changing these thoughts to positive input for our human computer.

Throughout history, certain people have shown themselves capable of leading others to achievement. These people seemed to possess some strange, inner quality in their personalities that made them appear strong, steady, and in control of themselves. They had the courage to attempt seemingly impossible things, and they usually attained the goals they set for themselves and the group. The greatness of their achievements may be duplicated by anyone who has mastered the seven principles of self-motivation. When the principles are applied, the results are amazing. They come to understand that their actions are the result of controlling the information that is fed to the human computer.

Getting yourself ready to deal with details, as well as with the larger picture, starts with waking up each day and thinking positive thoughts that will condition your mind and body for that entire day's action. Believe what you are thinking. When you have faith in your thoughts, positive currents of energy flow in your brain and body and make your actions dynamic, worthy, and powerful for the good of mankind. In explaining to others this plan for becoming self-motivated, you will receive great inspiration and positive creative energy. Fulfilling the desire to help others is a tremendously satisfying ingredient of success. Winning is wrapped up in motivation. The lesson brings forth the same message each time — belief. It works because of actions performed by the human computer. People of all ages have known about it, and those with wisdom have used it. Socrates, the Greek philosopher, regularly took his class out to the country by a lake. One day a young student asked Socrates how to attain wisdom. Socrates led the student down to the lake, pushed his head under the water, and held him there for several moments. The young lad, pushing and fighting to pull his head out of the water, screamed, "I asked you how I could find wisdom and you tried to drown me!" To which Socrates replied, "If you want wisdom as bad as you wanted air, you will find it." Wisdom can be taught to others through sincere thinking, clear writing, and simple language.

WE LEARNED FROM OTHERS

How do you use self-motivation to achieve career success? Our class learned from a number of people.

Carolyn Luesing, president and owner of her own company and a University of North Caroline graduate, is an expert on business etiquette and a favorite class speaker each year. Because the majority of class members are approaching graduation and anticipating entry into their careers, the lessons she teaches have a significant impact. She gives tips that not only aid in the interview process but that also can produce career success.

In business, projecting a professional, confident image and practicing the nuances of business etiquette are essential components of career success, she writes. Business etiquette is the art of appearing gracious and pointed, while at the same time making others feel comfortable. Dale Carnegie states that 85 percent of one's success will depend on interpersonal skills, including the ability to handle others with tact and style, and 15 percent will depend on technical skills. A courteous demeanor will advance your career and facilitate your interviewing process.

Etiquette is defined as respecting oneself and others, doing what is appropriate and acceptable, showing kindness and consideration, and behaving consistently with the Golden Rule. That rule, of course, is "Treat others as you would like to be treated." Good manners directly affect the bottom line in any economy and may be the deciding factor in whether a person is hired and retained in a job.

The following are some important areas of business etiquette to observe:

- Monitor conversation for business – avoid jokes, slang, acronyms, profanity, and gossip. Avoid personal topics, such as health, misfortunes, and sensitive subjects.

- Pay attention to introductions, greetings, and names.

- Use good listening skills and show interest in others.

- Practice the art of dining and entertaining. Be a good host and guest.

- Politely use cell phones, voice mail, email, phones, or pagers.

- Make a practice to write notes, send out only professional letters, and observe RSVPs to invitations.

- Practice punctuality in meetings, returning phone calls, and sending information.

- Be careful about alcoholic beverages in business situations.

In today's competitive business environment, paying attention to the details of business etiquette will enhance your ability to obtain job positions and to attract and retain customers in any job capacity, advises Luesing.

~

Students from the course interviewed Bud Shaw, a frequent guest speaker, regarding his concepts of positive leadership. Shaw and his brother Bob are the founders of Shaw Industries, the world's largest producer of carpets. With Shaw Industries, Bud was able to accomplish his personal goal to run a $40-million business by the age of forty. Shaw Industries relied on the strengths of its people, guided by the two brothers.

Bud Shaw feels that there are two types of people in business: the do-it-yourselfers and the delegators. The do-it-yourselfers are able to do only what their own two hands will allow them to do. The delegators are able to extend themselves through others to increase productivity. Success for a delegator depends on a relationship of trust. The leader must take the blame if a delegated job is not completed correctly and pass any received praise to his constituents for a job well done. The skill of finding those in whom you have confidence takes years of practice, and it is a trait that has been one of Bud Shaw's greatest strengths.

For example, in one division of his business, Shaw hired an individual with outstanding credentials and experience. However, upon closer inspection, that person's values and attitude were not suited to the situation, and the venture was unsuccessful. That experience taught Bud that attitude and values are more important than credentials. Shaw is a delegator by nature. He has a philosophy of keeping a "clean plate" – meaning, once a task presents itself and all of the facts are at hand, don't procrastinate: "Do it now."

Bud Shaw believes that every individual defines success differently. In his words, "My concept of success is defined in five parts: professional accomplishment so that my work has improved a chosen industry; community service that has added to others' quality of life; a healthy and happy family; fulfillment of personal goals; and a spiritual life that embraces both understanding and belief."

Following are several additional strategies and techniques Shaw has used in striving for success:

- "Procrastination is the greatest defeater of enthusiasm."

- "Eliminate your mistakes early; don't allow them to compound over time."

- "Admitting your mistakes forces integrity upon yourself."

- "Listen. It is the most important part of communication. Don't think instead about what you're going to say next."

- "I encourage every person to try to be in business for themselves. The backbone of America is people in business for themselves."

- "A financial background is essential for anyone in business."

- "Dare to compete, dare to fail. Athletics teaches you to put yourself on the line."

~

Martha Lanier, president of her own company called "Igniting Unlimited Potential," in her message to the class presented a point-by-point plan for successful, positive leadership:

- Live by choice as opposed to chance.
- Have a plan.
- Be specific.
- Break goals down into small segments.
- Put it in writing.

- Look at it everyday.
- Make it measurable.
- Have a time frame attached.
- Share your goals.
- Take time to review your progress.
- Utilize your strengths—mediocrity is useless.
- Strengthen strengths and delegate weaknesses.
- Have 3 Support Groups:
    1) Masterminds—like minded groups
    2) Advisory Board—support system
    3) Advocates—strengthen professionally
- Develop expertise and focus on solutions.
- Create your own belief system.

~

Hubert L. "Herky" Harris, Jr., chairman and Chief Executive Officer of INVESCO Retirement, Inc., served our country during the administration of President Jimmy Carter and spoke to the class on building success traits to become a positive leader.

His points:

- Luck—Sometimes, being in the right place affects our future.

- Integrity is something that can be easily lost and is very hard to regain.

- Aggressiveness—Figure out what your goal is and strive for it.

- Taking calculated risks—One must understand all of the consequences first.

- Having a keen sense of awareness—Know what is going on around you. Know the circumstances and understand human dynamics.

- Must have flexibility—Change is a fact of life.

- Must do your homework—The more you show you know about a certain person and their company, the more respect you will receive.

These seven principles were important elements in the success Herky Harris has achieved to this day.

~

John Williams founded Post Properties, Inc., and continues as chairman *emeritus* for that prestigious enterprise. He developed one of the most successful apartment-living communities in the United States by living his simple business philosophy. He describes it as "based on the concept of being more than fair — more than fair to customers, more than fair to associates, and more than fair to investors. And, finally, have fun. The work environment should be exciting, stimulating, and especially lots of fun."

~

Jack Markwalter is managing director and head of Client Services and Business Development for Atlanta Trust Company, NA. He has served in the past as managing director for Morgan Stanley and Company. Jack has also been a frequent guest as one of our top class speakers. He had phenomenal success in the business world but also is a total person as a family man. He possesses integrity, self-discipline, and high energy that have helped him reach the top of the ladder.

Jack graduated from Georgia Tech in 1981 before going to Harvard Business School for his MBA. I hired this young man to work for our Georgia Tech Athletic Association, and this is the story why:

In his senior year at Georgia Tech, Jack was actively involved and served as the student body president . During that time, many students were forced to live off campus in unsafe neighborhoods surrounding the campus. Students went to the Georgia State Board of Regents for funds, only to learn that the Regents had already allocated their entire annual budget. The only option left was to get money through the Board's supplementary funds. In order to do this, Jack organized a huge publicity campaign in which parents of every in-state student were called and asked to write letters to their representatives and other important legislators in the state of Georgia. In addition, he was able to get free television time from a local news station. His efforts eventually resulted in $18 million in state funds to build the new Woodruff Dormitory.

After Jack graduated from Tech, he worked for the Alexander-Tharpe Fund through the Georgia Tech Athletic Association to raise money for scholarships for athletes. During the time, Georgia Tech was rebuilding its athletic association. In order to make it one of the best in the nation, Tech needed to provide better opportunities to the athletes it was recruiting. While Jack worked with the Alexander-Tharpe Fund, the second largest amount of money for athletic scholarships in the nation was raised.

Through these experiences, Jack learned the following:

- Set high goals—anything is possible.
- Power of teamwork
- Surround yourself with great people.
- Reward, recognize, and motivate

- Lead by example.
- Power of positive thinking

He also included these thoughts on leadership:

- Vision
- Ethics and integrity
- Service orientation
- Communication skills
- Self awareness
- Teamwork

I would not be surprised someday to read the headline, "Jack Markwalter Elected Governor of Georgia." He is a successful, positive leader

~

Henry F. "Hank" McCamish, Jr., has been a close friend for many years. In the early 1970s, I put together a leadership seminar at the Pine Needles Golf and Country Club in Pinehurst, NC, at the request of Warren and Peggy Kirk Bell.

At the time, I was Director of Athletics at the University of North Carolina and had just co-authored *Leadership in Athletics* with my good friend, Paul Meyer. The purpose of the conference was to explore the "Total Person—Total Success" concept. Fortunately, I was successful in bringing in experts to lecture and discuss these topics—Paul Meyer, Dr. Ken Cooper, Carl Stevens, Jack Kinder, and Hank McCamish.

Hank and I remained close for years. We met again in 1980 when I moved to Georgia Tech. As we pursued the Total Person Program for student-athletes, Hank was instrumental in getting the program, and later a separate building, off the ground. He insisted on naming the new facility in my honor. I resisted, but in the end Hank won by saying, "No name, no check!" Hank has been ultra successful as a positive leader. The 50 points he stressed to the class in his lecture are worth whatever space is required to include them in *Leadership Fitness*. They appear in full as Appendix G.

~

Jim Lientz, former President of the Mid-South Bank of America, co-founder of the Triveritas Group, and now the state's first chief operating officer for Georgia Governor Sonny Perdue, made key points to the class about becoming a positive leader:

- Everybody is a leader of some kind: quiet, noisy, data driven, emotional/impulsive.

- Emulate the "Think 'Team' Orientation" of positive leaders – there is a reason we have two ears and one mouth.

- Trust your instincts.

- Genuinely care about people.

- Do what you say you are going to do.

- Leaders must be candid and specific.

- Be optimistic and take big chances. (Hugh McCall)

- Be a servant leader. (Governor Sonny Perdue)

- Spend time developing those around you.

- Leaders understand that there is plenty of success to go around.

- Leaders are typically happy and positive people.

- Be an intense competitor, but realize that no one wins 100 percent.

- Leaders don't have time for superficiality or surface people.

- Listen more than you talk.

- Leadership rights are extremely fragile.

~

Bill Curry, former gridiron leader and now an ESPN TV football analyst, spoke to the class about goal setting. Bill knew first-hand about our course. When I became director of athletics at Georgia Tech in 1980, Bill was our head football coach. To build our program, I taught this course to our staff and coaches. I might add that Bill was a prize student. His remarks reinforced to the class the lesson on goal setting (Lesson 8). He emphasized how self-motivation is the key to becoming a successful, positive leader, and he made a real impression on the class with his comments.

~

Jack Kinder of Kinder Brothers International Group, Inc., in Dallas, TX, is a sales management consultant to several hundred corporations. He is an expert on positive leadership. His years in management have taught him many things, but none more important than, "Managers manage things; leaders lead people."

The leader's challenge is to achieve both success and significance. This is accomplished when the leader makes a commitment to excellence, defines and steadfastly pursues an organizational vision, builds self-discipline, and lives his or her life in balance.

The leader consistently teaches lessons that stay taught. "Leadership," Kinder noted, "is a succession of lessons that must be lived to be understood."

~

The stories of all great leaders remind us that success is seldom accidental, according to Carl Stevens from Houston, TX, known as the "Creator of a College Education in Professional Selling."

As we all become "chronologically enhanced," it is interesting to reflect on what makes one individual more successful than another. What is your definition of success?

We can agree that the successful person is an individual who does what he or she has predetermined that they want to do and optimizes his or her innate abilities. In the process, everybody involved wins.

"You win with people," according to football coach Woody Hayes. What makes a super-successful winner or leader?

The successful, positive leaders Stevens has known and studied have unique qualities but common denominators. Positive leaders seem to understand these things:

1. The potential for communication magic with words. Some of us think of the late Dr. Norman Vincent Peale as a pioneer in the field of positive leadership. A personal letter Dr. Peale penned to Stevens about a manuscript reflects his elegance in writing. "It communicates most effectively and is devoid of pedantic phraseology that might bewilder the reader," he wrote.

Successful positive leaders don't bewilder their listeners. They inspire them.

2. In a recent survey, 72 percent of leaders said they did not have time to think or plan. A client and friend who sold the business he started immediately after high school for $4 million advised that, "A man needs time to ponder and plan."

3. If you had an IQ four points higher than Einstein, what advice would you give a would-be successful leader? Here's his counsel regarding decision-making. Evaluate each decision with this question: Will this choice help me reach my ultimate goal and objective?

4. Napolean Hill said that 98 percent of people fail because they have no chief aim or goal. Many leaders are ineffective. Peter Drucker said, "Being efficient is doing things well; being effective is doing the right things." A professional goal is a prerequisite to becoming an effective leader.

5. A wise author wrote, "Take time to think. It is the source of power. Take time to pray. It is the greatest power on earth."

In a survey of more than 500 business presidents and vice presidents, poor prioritizing was common. The survey reported that despite keeping long hours, only 47 percent of leaders' working time was taken up with leadership duties. They filled most of the remaining time with hands-on work, "doing" as opposed to "leading."

6. President Ronald Reagan was referred to as "The Great Delegator." He had a sign in his office that read, "It is amazing what you can accomplish if you don't care who gets credit for it." President Reagan told a *Time* magazine reporter that, "The highest grade I made in college was a C+." So you C+ students – maybe you, too, can become the leader of the free world.

The most successful, positive leaders I have known and studied seem to keep strict scores on themselves. They use benchmarks and keep a close watch on their continuing progress. Talk to yourself every hour, on the hour, to stay focused.

If we are not going to learn from history, why should we value it? Study and learn from the super leaders. A positive leader is a perpetual learner.

7. Critique yourself. At the end of each project and each day, do this: Invest five to ten minutes reconstructing the day, reviewing the key activities, and evaluating your strong and weak points. Ponder and enlist your subconscious to help you twenty-four hours a day!

Follow the lead of our nation's first great leader, General George Washington. Take time to pray. It is the greatest power on earth.

LESSON SEVEN

FINANCIAL INDEPENDENCE

TITHING, AND PROSPERITY

FINANCIAL INDEPENDENCE

Positive, successful leaders strive to be successful in all areas of their lives. They often begin with a spiritual commitment to following God's commandments. They build a positive self-image, seek optimal health, and achieve career success by means of self-motivation. And, finally, they reach financial independence. Some people seek only financial success, and material things become their benchmarks. However, true successful, positive leaders will always include all four areas of the total person-total success plan in their pursuit of real happiness.

It is important to plan to become financially independent by a certain age. We should plan so that our families will have all the things they need whether we live or die. We can do this through life insurance and careful investing. I suggest locating a good life insurance agent and looking into term-life insurance.

After that, build a portfolio through the years that consists of savings, investments, and real estate. I believe the larger part of the portfolio should be in fixed income, such as high-quality corporate bonds, municipal bonds, and U.S. treasury bonds with a broad range of maturity dates. In equities, look for stocks that pay dividends, have had high credit ratings for a long period of time, and represent goods or services that will be in demand and needed into the future. In investments, I believe in real estate. You have your home, a cottage at the beach or lake, and other properties. Then maintain these properties, upgrading periodically to increase the value. Wasn't it Will Rodgers who said of land, "They're not making any more of it"?

TITHING

One area that should never be neglected is tithing. A positive, successful leader should always give first to God's plan. Somewhere along my career route, I began taking 10 percent or more off the top of my gross income each month in order to tithe to my church and other charitable organizations. This is my seventh book. The first three dealt with football coaching and player techniques. The sales from those three books helped finance our three daughters through college.

The next three books were about leadership – particularly my Attitude Technique philosophy (total person-total success concept). The proceeds from those books were disbursed to charity, in addition to my planned tithing, and in most cases to causes that benefited young people. Being a giver brings much happiness and satisfaction. Amazingly, being a giver also has its rewards. I always receive much more than I ever expect from sources of which I never dreamed.

PROSPERITY

Prosperity came to me in various forms and through many people, but I always realized God was the source of all. While financial security may help us feel at ease, however, peace of mind can be found only through a relationship with God. Ezekiel 34:29-30: "I will provide for them so they shall no more be consumed with hunger in the land – they shall know that I, the Lord their God, am with them."

As I write this section, we are in the midst of a volatile market. We have experienced the tragedy of September 11, 2001, and the corporate scandals of 2002 — Enron, World-com, Global Crossing, and Arthur Anderson. The long war with terrorism, coupled with these scandals, affects how we respond and the adjustments we must make in future years. Therefore, making a positive plan must be a high priority.

During my early years as a young coach-teacher on the high school level, I struggled sometimes to make ends meet and to provide for my family. To compensate, I looked for other jobs during the off-season. Luck came my way when Ed Cassada, my former baseball manager, connected me with a part-time life insurance sales job. It was a blessing in many ways. I became a million-dollar salesman in six months and at the same time learned how to plan my finances for the future and set goals to become financially independent. This positive approach led me to read and study many books and programs on this subject.

SUGGESTED TITLES TO READ

Wealth and Poverty by George Gilder
The Power and Money Dynamics by Venita Vancaspel
Keep Your Wealth in the Family by Phillips Publishing, Inc.

How Much Am I Really Worth? By James P. Poole
The Prosperity Solution by Jonathan Parker
Building Financial Success by Paul Meyer's Success Motivation®
    International, Inc.
U.S. News and World Report – Money Management Library
Financial Genius by Mark Oliver Haroldsen
Free to Choose by Milton & Rose Friedman
The Complete Book of Personal Finance by Boardroom Classics
Personal Finance for Dummies by Eric Tyson
Charles Schwab's Guide to Financial Independence
The Millionaire Next Door by Tom Stanley and William Danko

Beyond your salary, commission fees, bonuses, etc., there are
other ways to earn income for your family and special needs as
long as they do not interfere with your position of leadership.
They may even complement what you do. I recommend speaking engagements, clinic lectures, writing, TV-radio shows, and
other related area. Do not overlook any possibilities.

Be certain to have a last will and testament, a letter of instructions, family budget, power of attorney, and all your investment
and business transactions in a portfolio in the event of your inca-
pacity to act or death. Seek the advice and help of a good friend
who has a background in economics and law to assist with your
planning. I was fortunate to meet such people who have helped
me significantly through the years. Rick Worsham, a friend with
an honors undergraduate degree from Georgia Tech in chemical
engineering and a law degree from the University of Virginia,
has helped me tremendously.

After being admitted to the State of Georgia Bar and receiving
his CPA certificate, Rick co-founded an Atlanta firm. He became
my personal financial advisor many years ago. With his advice
and counseling, I reached my planned, written goal to become
financially independent by a certain age. Rick has been a frequent

guest at my Leadership Fitness class at Georgia Tech. His lectures and materials have helped many of my students to embark upon their careers in the real world on a positive note. Following his steps will also aid you in becoming financially successful.

Rick says that during 30 years of working with hundreds of clients in the area of personal financial planning, he has found six key principles that, if adhered to, will vastly improve your overall quality of life and specifically ensure financial security and comfort:

1. Never incur "bad" debt.
2. Never compromise your values for the sake of money or things.
3. Create and revise, as needed, a long-term money plan.
4. If married, remember that your goals must reflect the interests both of you and your spouse.
5. Spending habits are the key to reaching financial goals.
6. Money does not bring happiness.

Here he expands on that advice, giving valuable pointers to us all.

1. Never incur "bad" debt. I'm not saying that one should never borrow money or that all debt is bad. Good debt, such as that used to buy a home or to fund a small business, is generally available at lower interest rates than "so-called" bad debt, such as credit cards, and it is usually tax-deductible. If properly and smartly managed, "good debt" purchases should also increase in value. Borrowing to pay for educational expenses can also make sense. Education is generally a good long-term investment, which should increase one's earnings potential.

Bad debt, on the other hand, is usually incurred for consumption. Striving for the "good life" always has been an integral part of the American Dream. But in recent years our lust for material possessions has spiraled out of control. Corporations have convinced us that what once were luxuries – large homes, SUVs and wide-screen TVs, for example – are now necessities. In previous generations, we looked to our neighbors and those with similar incomes and lifestyle aspirations for cues as to where we stood in the social hierarchy. These days, we often look to new reference groups for cues – athletes, overpaid celebrities, top executives, and "regular folks" in our TV shows – whose incomes may be many times our own. Advertisers, retailers, and even the "Joneses" next door exploit this new consumerism. They promote the illusion that all of us should live like wealthy people. Hence, we are encouraged to incur "bad debt" – the exorbitant, non-mortgage debt on credit cards or debt for luxury automobiles.

Every time you buy something, you have a choice whether to pay for it now or to charge it. The ease of charging an item is tempting, and you can rack up big bills without blinking an eye. Responsible use allows you to finance a purchase when cash is temporarily unavailable. But effective use of credit cards means paying off debt each month. Otherwise, you'll be paying interest at very high rates, in effect adding a significant amount to the price of each item you buy.

The "Rule of 72," which can be used to determine the number of years it will take for your investment to double in value or your debt to double in size, is a good tool to illustrate this point. It works this way: divide the number 72 by the percentage rate you are paying on your debt or earning on your investment. Here is an example. You borrow $1,000 at an 18 percent credit card interest rate. Divide 72 by 18, and you get four. That means that in four years your debt will double to $2,000 if you do not have any principal reduction. Remember: 72 divided by the interest percentage equals the number of years the initial investment or debt takes to double. (You can also use 115 to determine how long the amount takes to triple.)

If you have a problem with credit cards, cut them up or put them away. If you have built up credit card debts, establish goals to pay them off as fast as possible. Think analytically regarding automobile purchases. If you must have a new car, take advantage of zero-percent financing. Otherwise, interest paid on the car loan results in raising the effective price of the automobile to much more than the original purchase price (on an asset that will incur considerable loss in value once you drive it off the dealer's lot). The purchase of a used vehicle (or keeping a new vehicle for a longer period of time) is financially prudent. Holding each car you buy for 10 years can result in savings of as much as $400,000 over your lifetime.

Good debt is debt incurred for the purchase of your home. Real estate investments should be part of your total investment portfolio. A sound formula for mortgage loans is that the total annual debt should be less than or equal to 38 percent of household income, and that home mortgage annual debt, plus property taxes and home insurance, should be less than or equal to 28 percent of income.

2. Never compromise your values for the sake of money or things. Despite overwhelming evidence to the contrary, most people still believe that money brings happiness, and some will do almost anything to attain more money, which allows them to get more things. To quote the Apostle Paul in his first letter to Timothy in the New Testament, "Godliness with contentment is great gain, ... but people who want to get rich fall into temptation and a trap and into many foolish and harmful desires that plunge people into ruin and destruction. For the love of money is the root of all kinds of evil. Some people, eager for money, have wandered from faith and pierced themselves with many griefs." (I Timothy 6:6-10) The happiness that money and things bring is short lived and fleeting. Additionally, compromised values have a huge range of effects – anything from feeling down (because a value system is innate to the human psyche) to criminal charges, if laws are broken to attain more dollars (consider all of the recent corporate scandals).

3. Create and revise, as needed, a long-term money plan. Make sure to take time to write your goals. A study done at a Yale University 20-year class reunion found that only three percent of the class had written goals. Interestingly, the combined net worth of those who had written goals was greater than that of the remaining 97 percent who didn't. Writing expenditures allows you to see how much money is spent on discretionary items, such as new clothes, new cars, unnecessary travel, or expensive and destructive habits such as smoking and drinking. If you cut spending on nonessentials and invest that money making eight percent, you can save surprising amounts. Saving $1.50 a day on junk food, alcohol, or tobacco from age 18 to age 67 results in an extra $290,373. Also, a written plan will allow you to see how much you are paying in credit card interest, if you do not pay off your credit cards on a monthly basis. Maintaining credit card debt is one of the most destructive and sure-fire ways to derail your monetary and personal goals. As you develop your financial plan, keep in mind that it's important to be realistic – unrealistic goals will lead to only frustration (remember the Rule of 72). You must recognize that your goals may change and that you'll need to review them regularly to keep your financial plan on course in the face of shifting economic, political, and personal winds.

4. If married, remember that your goals must reflect the interests of both you and your spouse. A written plan will allow you to identify the differences in attitudes between you and your spouse. Alignment of your goals with the goals of your spouse is a major key to personal success. For example, if one spouse wants to put extra money each month towards the purchase of a second home and the other towards funding the children's college education, tension will result. Plans and objectives must be discussed and agreements then reached for effective financial planning and goal attainment. Once you've set your goals, the next step in the personal financial planning process is to figure out how to accomplish these goals, given your income level and net worth. It's at this stage that most people can benefit from the help of a professional financial manager to develop financial strategies for the long term to meet their goals. But it's important to be aware of the pieces that make up any sound financial plan: cash flow analysis; savings; retirement plans and funding; investment strategy (with a rule of thumb being 100 minus your age as the percentage of your investment portfolio that should be invested in stocks); insurance (a rule of thumb is that a married couple should have life insurance coverage in the amount of 10 times the amount of annual income); and estate planning. A financial planner (CFP or CPA/PFS) is equipped to address each of these issues.

5. Spending habits are key to reaching financial goals. I mentioned this earlier when talking about credit cards and discretionary spending, but it is so important in achieving financial goals that it must be highlighted as a key principle. If you are currently in a position where your spending is out of control and/or debts are unmanageable, you need to seek counseling or attend Debtors Anonymous (www.debtorsanonymous.org), if necessary, to align your spending habits and your goals.

As part of the written plan, you need to analyze your cash flow. Find out how much you actually spend each month. It's easy to keep track of the large expenses such as mortgage, tuition, and insurance payments. On the other hand, the more variable items such as food, clothing, and entertainment cause the most surprises. If you are at a loss as to where your money is going, keep track of what you spend for several months or longer, if necessary. Personal budgeting software such as Quicken or Managing Your Money can make this process easier. Compare this cash-outflow figure with your monthly income. If you find that your cash in-flow matches or exceeds your outflow, it's time to start living below your means. Determine which part of your spending is discretionary and start reining it in.

Living below your means is the only way to save for the future. Saving is one of those things that almost everyone thinks is a good idea but that few people actually commit to. You know the excuses – not enough income, too many bills, too many investing options, and on and on. An easy way to get started is to pay yourself first from each income check. Decide on a percentage of your income (10 percent is a good rule of thumb) to put into a savings account or into an employer-sponsored account. If you put money into a savings account, you can then move the money in larger chunks from the savings account into other investment options on a regular basis. The laws of compounding interest are truly amazing. Using the "Rule of 72" or "115," you can quickly calculate how fast your money will double or triple. Divide 72 or 115 by the expected annual rate of return to determine how many years it will take to double and triple your money. Another rule of thumb is that you should have three to six months worth of living expenses saved as a personal safety net for emergencies. If you are self-employed, you should set up a business contingency fund, as well as a personal savings net.

6. Money does not bring happiness. Of course, neither does poverty. But unmanageable debt can bring great pain! After working with hundreds of clients on money issues over the last thirty years, I've concluded that some of the unhappiest people are wealthy ones who have isolated themselves from friends and family in order to attain wealth. The role of money in happiness is somewhat mystical, in that the amount of money required for happiness differs greatly from person to person. The one constant fact I have learned is that money must be blended with the proper amount of family, friends, personal goals, charity, and spirituality to produce happiness. All must be present, but the amount and nature of the blend differs with each person.

Thanks to Rick Worsham for sharing this information that will benefit each of us!

LESSON EIGHT

THE GOALS PROGRAM

Throughout this book, my message has been *write it down* – there is magic in writing your thoughts. Doing so will help you to change negatives to positives, defeats to victories, and bad or wrong thoughts to good and wholesome thoughts.

We may struggle with our thoughts – doing the right or wrong thing – but it's a simple matter of choice. By controlling our thoughts, and with God's help, we can strengthen the good side by planting the right seeds within the human computer.

Remember: Your thoughts are being processed inside your human computer, and whatever is received will determine your actions and the type of person you will eventually become. Therefore, to succeed in any undertaking, it's imperative to set a goal, and that process must start with a written commitment clearly defined. Don't be concerned with minute details in the beginning – should changes be necessary, you can make them later. Just starting is the most important step. Follow the plan and you will receive whatever you are seeking, as long as it is realistic and within your capabilities. However, shoot for the top – do not settle for an easy goal that can be reached without a tremendous effort.

GOAL ORIENTED FOR GOOD THINGS IN LIFE!

Some people can picture what they want and go get it without writing their desires – they simply keep their mind's eye on the object and continually push toward their goal until it is completed. Unfortunately, most people are like me. If they want to reach a goal, they must systematically write it, read it aloud each day, and keep written score of their progress until the goal is reached. Written motivation forces us to persevere until we get there.

Regardless of which type you are, once the goal is reached you cannot rest and wallow in victory – you must set another goal to keep from sliding backward. Amazingly, only about five percent of our world's population attempts either approach. And sadly, some people use the technique for evil ends. Positive, worthwhile, ethical, and meaningful values of life must regain center stage for the good of all people. Since only about five percent are really trying to reach worthwhile goals, it's apparent that the field is wide open for anyone to step up and succeed. Ninety-five percent of people are not even attempting to become successful and fulfill a higher purpose in life to benefit others and themselves.

The seven steps in acquiring your goal are:
- Commitment
- Target Date
- Ingredients
- Giving
- Visualization
- Belief and Expectancy
- Positive Prayer

Goals can be categories for the short term, long term or any length of time. Once you have a goal clearly defined and written, it becomes your commitment. This does not mean that you cannot change the phrasing from time to time. But remember that once the goal is set, the action begins. This is your first step. Don't wait. The sooner you write your goal, the faster it will become a reality. Should you think or say, "I can't do this," you are probably right; your human computer picks up your thoughts and agrees with you. It will perform whatever action you give it. Be bold. Change that negative attitude to positive thoughts, and your human computer will perform as you have ordered.

After completing step one, set a deadline – a target date by which you intend to reach your goal. If the goal is to be accomplished in five, 10, or 20 years, that's a long-term goal. If it is something you want in a year or less, it is a short-term goal. I am often asked, "What do I do if the goal is not reached within the time period I set?" My reply is always the same: "Re-set the target date and move on." As you work through the seven-step process and look at your written goal on a daily basis, it may change as new and better ideas develop. Creatively will always come into play.

Once your commitment and target date are recorded, move to step three —ingredients: "What will it take to reach my goal?" Again, write the procedures. You may need to discuss your goal with others, or go to the library and research the subject or any procedures necessary to attain the goal. Remember to record these "ingredients" and look at them daily; then erase, add, or subtract necessary information that will lead you to the action. This step becomes a motivational force toward your commitment. Another friend and frequent speaker to the students of Leadership Fitness is Russ Chandler. His success in life stems from his strong commitment. In Appendix H, he explains the philosophy that has sustained him.

Step four is giving — What are you willing to give in return for what you will receive? We must give before we receive. As I mentioned before, there are two classes of people — the "grabbers" and the "givers." Scientists have discovered that a person of generous spirit generally enjoys a longer life span than a person focused on "taking and grabbing." Helping others reach their goals will increase your capacity to have what you are seeking.

The fifth step is visualization. You must visualize your goal as being already completed. Mentally, you must have in your possession what you are seeking. Remember: Your human computer will accept whatever you imagine. It does not distinguish between what is real and what is imagined. It accepts what you think and feel; it allows information to pass from the conscious to the subconscious.

The builder visualizes the type of building he wants. He sees the structure as he desires it to be completed. His imagination and thought processes become a mold from which the building will emerge. His mental imagery is projected as it is drawn on paper. Eventually, the contractor and his workers gather the essential materials and the building progresses until finished, conforming perfectly to the mental patterns of the architect. A mental picture held in the mind, backed by faith, will come to pass.

Repeating an affirmation – knowing what you are saying and why you are saying it – leads the mind to that state of consciousness where it accepts the statement as truth.
This procedure will help you reach your goal because you can actually see it happening. Here's a wonderful story about never losing sight of your goal:

Florence Chadwick wanted to be the first woman ever to swim the English Channel. For years she trained to reach her goal, disciplining herself to keep going long after her body cried out for relief. Finally the big day arrived. She set after her goal, full of hope, surrounded by the press and well-wishers. Things went well, but as she neared the coast of England, a heavy fog settled in and the waters became increasingly cold and choppy. "Come on, Florence," her mother encouraged her from a nearby boat as she handed her food. "You can make it! It's only a few more miles!"

Then, not realizing she was within a few hundred yards of her goal, Chadwick became completely exhausted and asked to be pulled into the boat. She was defeated and heartbroken, especially when she discovered how close she had been to reaching her goal. She told reporters, "I'm not offering excuses, but I think I could have made it if I had been able to see my goal."

Later, like a true winner, she bounced back from her temporary failure and tried again. This time she concentrated on developing a mental image of the English coastline. She memorized every feature of the distant coast and held it clearly in mind. When the big day arrived, she again encountered the fog and the cold, choppy waters. This time, however, she reached her goal. She became the first woman in history to swim the English Channel. She accomplished what she had set out to do because she could visualize her goal. Even when she could not see anything, her goal was always in focus in her human computer.

The sixth step is belief and expectancy. If we do not truly believe and have absolute faith, our goal may not be reached. Our progress will stop right there, and we will be at a dead end. We must keep saying, "I believe, I believe," all the while keeping positive thoughts flowing into the human computer. By writing out positive thoughts or beliefs, we make our subconscious respond positively. Refuse to let negative thoughts of doubt enter the human computer. Change them, and you will become self-confident and the goal will be secured. Once a goal becomes a reality, you will then start expecting success time and time again. We can control our thoughts and, in turn, control our actions to acquire whatever it is we seek.

The seventh and last step is positive prayer, which constantly should be a major part of your thoughts. God allows us to seek and select whatever we want in life. If it benefits others, such as family, friends, or those in need, God will smile on the project and bless us. We should ask in prayer for God's guidance and blessings for what we are seeking. This should be a daily exercise. As we study the bible of God's lessons and teachings, we learn to find the strength to tackle any obstacle. I would even recommend that you write out your prayers. In this way, your written thoughts provide a path to follow. "You will succeed in all you do, and light will shine on your path." (Job 22-28)

More than 90 percent of your mental life is subconscious, so people who fail to control their subconscious minds also fail to control their lives. Your human computer is the builder of your body and maintains all of its vital functions. It is on the job twenty-four hours a day. It is always trying to help you and to protect you from harm.

The highest aspirations, inspirations, and visions for a nobler life spring from this inner power. Your most profound convictions are those you cannot argue about rationally because they do not come from the conscious mind. They come from the subconscious.

Your human computer speaks to you in impulses, hunches, urges, and ideas. It is always telling you to rise, grow, advance, seek adventure, and move forward to greater heights. Great artists, musicians, speakers, writers, and coaches tune in with their subconscious power, become animated, and experience inspiration. Mark Twain confided to the world on many occasions that he never worked in his life. All his humor and great writings were due to the fact that he tapped the inexhaustible reservoir of his subconscious mind.

The interaction of your conscious and subconscious minds requires a similar interplay between the corresponding systems of nerves. The cerebrospinal system is the organ of the subconscious mind. It is the channel. "As you sow, so shall you reap."

Now it is time to begin organizing your written goals. The following charts will aid you in this very significant and exciting undertaking. Make extra copies of these. Keep each goal in a notebook that you can work on daily. Spending just a few minutes each day will charge you positively and energize you for the day. Unbelievable results will occur. Just think – what you are beginning today will actually become your reality.

To enhance this process, follow a step-by-step approach. After writing on the goal sheet, make sure to read your goal aloud. This will connect the work you have done to your human computer. Behind each goal page is a worksheet that will aid you in making progress toward the finished project. You will undoubtedly encounter obstacles and roadblocks along the way. Note these encounters on the appropriate worksheet. This process will help you to understand clearly what problems (opportunities) exist. By understanding these, you can find a solution and turn the negative problem into a positive opportunity.

The written enlightens the clear path to a successful conclusion. Keep score on your daily actions, activities, and progress. And do not overlook noting the benefits you will enjoy. Your visualization and affirmations will sustain your high motivation.

MY SHORT-RANGE GOAL

1. I want _____

2. I want this goal fulfilled by _____

3. Necessary ingredients to obtain my goal:

_____
_____
_____
_____
_____
_____
_____

4. I will give in return:

_____
_____
_____
_____
_____
_____

5. I can visualize myself:

_____
_____
_____
_____
_____
_____

6. I believe and expect:

_____

_____

_____

_____

_____

_____

_____

_____

_____

7. My Positive Prayer today is:

_____

_____

_____

_____

_____

_____

_____

_____

_____

Read this Short-Range Goal aloud each day.

GOALS PLANNING FORM WORKSHEET

GOAL

TARGET DATE

OBSTACLES & ROADBLOCKS I MAY ENCOUNTER	SOLUTIONS TO OVERCOMING OBSTACLES	DATE I WILL TAKE ACTION	KEEPING SCORE ON MY ACTIVITIES

DATE AND PROGRESS MADE	BENEFITS I WILL ENJOY	VISUALIZATIONS	AFFIRMATIONS

MY LONG-RANGE GOAL

1. I want _____

2. I want this goal fulfilled by _____

3. Necessary ingredients to obtain my goal:

_____

_____

_____

_____

_____

_____

_____

4. I will give in return:

_____

_____

_____

_____

_____

_____

_____

5. I can visualize myself:

_____

_____

_____

_____

_____

_____

_____

6. I believe and expect:

_____

_____

_____

_____

_____

_____

_____

_____

_____

7. My Positive Prayer today is:

_____

_____

_____

_____

_____

_____

_____

_____

_____

Read this Long-Range Goal aloud each day.

GOALS PLANNING FORM WORKSHEET

GOAL

TARGET DATE

OBSTACLES & ROADBLOCKS I MAY ENCOUNTER	SOLUTIONS TO OVERCOMING OBSTACLES	DATE I WILL TAKE ACTION	KEEPING SCORE ON MY ACTIVITIES

DATE AND PROGRESS MADE	BENEFITS I WILL ENJOY	VISUALIZATIONS	AFFIRMATIONS

Lesson Nine

YOUR HIGH PURPOSE IN LIFE
AND KEEPING SCORE

We have talked about how to achieve short-term goals and long-term goals. Now let's talk about how to achieve the ultimate goal – finding our high purpose in life.

This may not be anything tangible. It may be something that can never be completely achieved but will bring peace of mind as we work on it for the rest of our lives. It may even be something that will carry on after your death. It's purpose – our purpose – is to make a difference in the world we live in.

Sound simple? Maybe, but it becomes complex because of circumstances we face each day. The first step is becoming a giver, not a grabber. (I recommend that you read and study Rick Warren's book, *The Purpose Driven Life ... What on Earth Am I Here For?*)

Your high purpose should be something that will influence others in a positive, wholesome way. My high purpose is sharing the Attitude Technique philosophy through the classes I teach, lectures, seminars, workshops, articles, manuscripts, coaching, and administration as a positive leader. Amazingly, many people write to me about this philosophy that has helped them to become positive leaders. As successful leaders, they now share the program with others. In mathematics, we call this multiplying!

That positive feedback keeps me going. I am compelled to continue this work. In fact, I want it to continue forever. With my close friend Bud Parker, I am considering creation of a foundation that will continue educating people about the Attitude Technique Philosophy even after my death. I have seen the remarkable results. It is worth every ounce of effort to press onward.

After Lesson One, you were asked to rate yourself on the Keeping Score chart. Let's repeat the exercise. On that chart, you should now be able to change many of the liabilities (weaknesses) into assets (strengths). Make extra copies of the chart and repeat this exercise often. The process will help you grow into the positive leader you desire, day by day.

Once you have completed and updated the Keeping Score chart, begin to discern your ultimate goal using the My High Purpose form. Make extra copies so that you can alter and update it from time to time.

This course is your guide to becoming a successful, positive leader. It can be your personal blueprint for a life of success, happiness, maturity, and growth. You will become a leader who emphasizes trust over cynicism, generosity over selfishness, and making people light up rather than being turned off. As time passes, you will be able to rearrange and adjust this program to your ongoing circumstances. You will be able to control your destiny with a highly organized mind, self-motivation, goal planning, and, above all, your communication with God through positive prayer. The Attitude Technique is a survival kit packaged and ready for action.

This program is real. Your goals can be achieved. You will develop positive leadership. Both you and others will be the beneficiaries. Above all, you will be fit to lead.

KEEPING SCORE

Rate: Superior, Excellent, Good, Fair, or Poor

Then Go Back and Write in Your Remarks

Subject	Assets (Strengths)	Liabilities (Weaknesses)
Spiritual Values		
Family Relations		
How I Perceive Myself		
How I Think Others Perceive Me		
Social Life		
How I Get Along With Others		
Health Status		
Aerobic Fitness		

Subject	Assets (Strengths)	Liabilities (Weaknesses)
Relaxation		
Recreational		
Rest		
Mental Stimulation		
Self-Discipline		
Self-Motivation		
Self-Confidence		
Controlled Visualization		
Goal Setting		
Career		
Financial Planning		

MY HIGH PURPOSE

I have these unique talents and abilities that I can use to contribute something worthwhile to the world:

_____

_____

_____

_____

_____

_____

_____

I will influence others:

1. To realize their full potential.
2. To set worthwhile and high goals in life.
3. To develop a positive mental attitude.
4. To practice the total person concept

This purpose is a great human need. I have found the answer to fill that need, and I will render a service to those who need it.

This high purpose will be good for my family and will give me personal satisfaction.

I will fulfill my commitment to this high purpose by accomplishing these goals:

_____

_____

_____

_____

MY ULTIMATE GOAL

1. I want _____

2. I want this goal fulfilled by _____

3. Necessary ingredients to obtain my goal:

_____

_____

_____

_____

_____

_____

_____

4. I will give in return:

_____

_____

_____

_____

_____

_____

_____

5. I can visualize myself:

_____

_____

_____

_____

_____

_____

_____

6. I believe and expect:

_____
_____
_____
_____
_____
_____
_____
_____
_____

7. My Positive Prayer today is:

_____
_____
_____
_____
_____
_____
_____
_____
_____

Read this Ultimate Goal aloud each day.

AFTERWORD

Great leaders are not born; they make their way. They may stumble at times, but they are able to adjust, start again, and continue until they develop a plan of action to lead. They may not be "perfect," but they will always strive toward positiveness by understanding and exercising the *right thing to do*!

Successful positive leaders have a vision, a mission, that can be explained clearly and concisely to their associates. They knit their group into a team, instilling trust in those who follow and forming a "family" that functions together. If we get the player right, the team will be right. The team does it!

At some time almost everyone has the opportunity or is put into a position to lead others. What a great challenge we have to emphasize the positive approach. This one word – *positive* – can make our group, our team, our country, and even the world a better place to live, work, and play.

From our class speakers and others, we have had the opportunity to listen and observe the characteristics that shape their positive leadership. Successful, positive leaders come from all walks of life. From the boating industry came Eddie Smith, owner of the Grady-White Boat Company in Greenville, North Carolina. In the late 1960s, I accepted a position as director of athletics at the University of North Carolina. One of my first assignments involved speaking to a UNC alumni group in Greenville. Eddie Smith, an alumnus of UNC, and his lovely wife, Jo, invited me to spend the night in their home. The next morning, Eddie drove me to an old building that was once a tobacco barn and explained that was the site where Grady-White boats were manufactured. As we drove along, Eddie explained that his desire to design a vehicle for customer comfort had prompted him to purchase the company. The customer came first!

Thirty years later, Eddie Smith was inducted into the Hall of Fame of the National Marine Manufacturers Association. His company is recognized and ranked highest in customer satisfaction by J.D. Powers and Associates. The Grady-White Boat Company became the most respected and admired boat company in the boating industry.

Eddie Smith succeeded to such a high level because he possesses the good qualities of a positive leader: integrity, dedication, and self-motivation. He is a true giver to others —to his "family of employees," but most of all to his customers. Regard for employees and especially for customers has led Eddie down the path of successful leadership.

~

During my early years as Director of Athletics at Georgia Tech, I met Bill Moore, founder and chairman of the board of Kelly-Moore Paint Company in San Carlos, California. Bill grew up the son of a barber in a small community in Arkansas. As a lad, he shined shoes at his father's barbershop to save money to attend college. His mother encouraged him to play tennis. The two activities paved the way to college when Georgia Tech offered him a partial scholarship. The scholarship was only a small portion of the cost, but Bill held down several other jobs to make it through the tough years following the Great Depression in our country.

In 1938, Bill graduated with a degree in Chemical and Industrial Engineering. He also led Georgia Tech to a Southeastern Conference tennis championship, never losing a match. After the All-American served in the Pacific Theater during World War II, he married his lovely wife Desiree and opened a paint company out of their garage. With Desiree at his side, he managed the privately-owned company that, in time, became the largest and most successful paint firm in the nation. His commitment to excellence and fairness paved the way for the company to be recognized throughout the United States. He was known as a man of high character in America's business community — a man of trust and integrity, and one who always did the right thing. His concern for the customer, his many innovations, continual growth and concern for excellence in every detail made his company flourish.

Bill Moore, a "giver," contributed the funds to build the Student Success Center at Georgia Institute of Technology, a facility dedicated to the students. In a talk to my class, he told the students, "May each find the foundation for a successful life: a positive balance of mind, body, and spirit."

In 1988, Bill purchased the Broken O Ranch in Augusta, Montana. At the time, the ranch consisted of almost 62,000 acres. By 1995, Bill Moore had grown the venture to 160,000 acres, making it the largest irrigated ranch in the state, comprising 200 square miles located in three counties.

As a frequent guest to fly fish the beautiful Sun River and Lowry Lake on that ranch's land, I became aware of another positive leader. Bill Moore hired Dan Freeman as president and general manager of the Broken O Ranch. I observed this man and his characteristics in developing the ranch to Moore's high expectations.

Being a leader of a vast area that contains thousands of cattle and buffalo and a farm division consisting of principle crops of wheat, malt barley, alfalfa, canola oil, and oats, required a man highly skilled and respected by the workmen. Knowledge and wisdom were also required to manage such an operation. Some days I traveled with Dan to get a firsthand view of the operation. It was immense – the cattle division, farm division, feed lot, cattle sale, harvesting, grain storage, irrigation systems, and crop rotation. Workers operated equipment from combines to bi-directional tractors, kept up with the many miles of fencing and, with the gravel on the premises, maintained 70 miles of roadway for connecting all of these operations.

A constant battle for water rights exists in Montana, where it is said that "whiskey is for drinking, water is for fighting." The seasons determine what work must be accomplished. Fall: shipping cattle, harvesting grain, draining the 69 pivots, and taking inventory of the crops scheduled. Winter: transporting grains to market, preparing equipment for spring, and the ongoing chore of feeding cattle and buffalo. Spring: calving, seeding crops, assembling pivots for irrigation. Summer: working crops, moving cattle to grassy fields and buffalo to fields with high fences, and developing a financial plan to turn a profit for the coming year.

Dan Freeman managed all of this. He also demonstrated the attributes of a positive leader with his family, workers, ranch hands, community, and church. Undoubtedly, he is a successful positive leader.

~

Whether on a ranch or at a major research university, just who is leading becomes quickly clear. Georgia Tech's President G. Wayne Clough is always a big hit with the class each year when he visits. His guidance of a major university is a real-life example to the students of what it takes to be a successful, positive leader. He set goals to guide Georgia Tech into the 21st Century as a world-class institution.

In his recent lecture to the class, he emphasized the importance of building a strong staff. The people on his teams measured up to the characteristics he looked for when assembling the teams. Those attributes include passion, diligence, expertise, loyalty, integrity, diversity, and optimism. It can be said that President Clough advanced Georgia Tech from the ranks of "good" to "great." His concern for long-run sustainability was evident. His expertise as a problem solver was clear, and he never failed to give credit to the team and its ability to achieve several goals – first, being proactive, reactive and decisive; second, being self-aware of strengths and weaknesses; and third, being complimentary to one another. A positive plan for the future, maintaining a team to carry out the goals set forth, and being proactive for change when change is needed – in addition to unbelievable fund raising ability – reflect his success and positive leadership.

GREAT SUCCESSFUL POSITIVE LEADERS OF

- Nations
- Militaries
- Corporations
- Teams
- Groups
- Religions
- Medicine
- Education
- Inventions

POSSESS CERTAIN QUALITIES AND SKILLS!

- Vision
- Tough decision-making abilities
- Communication, relating to others, being a good listener
- Surrounded by "positive" people who have been hired or appointed.
- Character, integrity, and respect

- High moral standards; a master of persuasion
- Self-motivation
- Effectiveness

After you leave or step down from a position, your positive results will be remembered!

~

Leadership fitness is the base of successful, positive leadership. Whatever field you are engaged in or about to enter will require study and skills to accomplish your goals. However, it is absolutely essential that you shape your life first.

In *Tech Topics*, Georgia Tech's news publication for alumni and friends, Maria M. Lameiras reported how Andrés Núñez followed the example of the Total Person program in creating his business:

> Andrés "Andy" E. Núñez, Jr., knows what it is like to work for a company that doesn't see its employees as key to its success. That is why Núñez, principal and co-founder of TEI Engineers & Planners, took a page from former Georgia Tech athletics director Homer Rice's playbook in running his own company.
>
> "Happy employees are more likely to stay. We invest a lot of time, effort and money into developing our employees and helping them to have a meaningful career," Núñez said. "We've pursued things that we would have liked some of our employers to do for us. Not to steal from Homer Rice, but we admire the companies who are doing that because it gives you a 'total person' experience."
>
> Núñez, who earned his bachelor's and master's degrees in civil engineering at Georgia Tech, founded TEI Engineers

& Planners in 1991. Since then, the company has won major awards, including TEI's designation as one of the "Top 100 Companies for Working Families" by the *Orlando Sentinel*.

TEI provides engineering consulting services including traffic engineering, transportation planning, traffic signal system design and implementation. It also specializes in roadway and highway design. The company has a strong community service component that Núñez said is largely directed by employees.

"We've set up a committee of employees who work independently and discuss the charities and activities they are interested in supporting, and we have usually gone with their recommendations," Núñez said. "We are not just dictating, 'Thou shalt do this or that.' We want them to be involved in what they are interested in. We are very active in those activities to show leadership – not just saying things, but doing them."

The company's Philanthropic Committee's mission is to make a positive difference in the lives of individuals and families by improving the environmental, economic, social, education and cultural prosperity of the communities in which they live and work. Those communities value the company's contributions, as evidenced by the many awards the firm has received.

TEI was named Central Florida's 2001 "Organization of the Year" in the large firm category and was ranked 15th among the nation's "Top 50 Best Engineering Firms to Work for" by *Civil Engineering News* magazine. The Seminole County/Lake Mary Regional Chamber of Commerce ranked the company, which has Florida offices in Lake Mary, Tampa, Tallahassee, Fort Lauderdale and Sarasota as well as in Atlanta, Georgia, among the "Top 25 Companies in Seminole County."

"You have to be forward thinking to get something off the ground – starting with nothing and creating what we have today," Núñez said. "The awards we have won for excellence and employee satisfaction have validated that we must be doing something right."

~

As this manuscript was being prepared for publication late in December 2003, the Leadership Fitness Class at Georgia Tech completed the fall semester. Each member of the class completed the coursework and an individual term project in order to become part of this manuscript for *Leadership Fitness*. Their research, interviews of contributors to the book, notes from guest speakers, and suggested changes, additions, and phrasing enriched this text on its way to publication.

I encourage you to do as my students have done – change words or phrasing to fit the particulars to your situation. Do so until the plan reflects *your* thoughts and *your* principles. Working through this manuscript until it becomes your personal blueprint for your life will create results.

Through the study of leadership fitness, guest speakers, interviews, informational research to obtain facts, and other friends of mine, the class of 2003 had the opportunity to express their personal reflections. As the class members wrapped up their reflections on the speakers, content, and their personal plans for the future, Lauren Weatherly, my effective teaching assistant and a graduating senior, compiled highlights of the class members' findings.

"Each fall, Coach Homer Rice gives his time and effort to a Leadership Fitness class for Georgia Tech students," wrote Lauren. "The students work through the concepts in this book, become inspired by incredible speakers each week, dine together, and learn an unbelievable amount from Coach Rice and the other students in these intimate settings. The students gain appreciation for the leadership techniques of Coach Rice, the history of Georgia Tech, and the importance of giving back as Coach Rice has done. Members of the class offered to share the following lessons they learned from the course:"

> *I believe the material covered in this course is more valuable than any other course I will take as an undergraduate student at Georgia Tech. Developing and reinforcing leadership skills is invaluable to me. I will be able to use these skills through all aspects of life: in school, business, family, etc. The concepts taught in this class set a foundation for leading a successful life.*
> – Andrea Inguanti

> *The Leadership Fitness class that I participated in this fall has been one of the best experiences of my life. Through the use of Dr. Rice's soon-to-be-published book,* Leadership Fitness, *I was able to learn more about leadership and living a positive life. I think the class has made me look more at the big picture for after graduation and the amazing possibilities I could be a part of after college.*
> – Jeff Rosenfeld

> *In my third year of college, I am starting to feel that I am gaining more direction in what I would like to pursue in a career and how I am going to get there. I grew up in a Buddhist family, and one main principal of this faith is to live in the present moment. Having this class was a great opportunity to have time to reflect and set*

goals in the midst of a busy college schedule. I feel that I am able to accomplish this more now than ever before, and I hope to continue to do so.
                                        – Paul Supawanich

The content of this class was phenomenal. The information presented through the chapters of Leadership Fitness *was truly inspirational and motivational. It really helped to put my life in the right perspective. I always left class realizing that the little things that frustrate and bother me are not really important. What is important is people and being able to make a difference in the lives of others.*
                                        – Jennifer Thornton

I can honestly say that this class was overwhelming. Typically when I say that about a class, I am talking about workload or overbearing professors. This class was a different type of overwhelming – the type where at times you feel an overabundance of joy. I cannot thank Coach Rice enough for his dedication to impressing upon our souls the qualities necessary to be a positive force in others' lives. I will take away more from this class than all of my previous courses combined.
                                        – Ellen Neidlinger

I want to thank Coach Rice for sharing his experiences with me through the class. I viewed his class as "free inspiration" and would always come up with my best ideas directly following class. The class made me think and helped motivate me. This program gives a unique chance for undergraduates at Tech to think outside the box as they take a break from their vigorous classes to think about more important items. This class provides the chance for students to ponder as well as to learn the importance of balance and leadership.

— Monique Gupta

I was extremely pleased with my experience in the Leadership Fitness class this fall. I always left the class excited and energized, and I definitely feel that I have grown as a leader and as a person by working through the notebook and interacting with such dynamic leaders. This class has been a fantastic experience, an opportunity to learn and explore ourselves under Coach Rice's guidance.

— Ben Lawder

This class has been the experience of a lifetime. I have thoroughly enjoyed getting to meet some of the most amazing Georgia Tech alumni that have graced the campus, as well as the amazing friends and colleagues of one of the most important figures in Georgia Tech history. I have been profoundly changed by this course. It gives me encouragement that when I sit down and plan and make the commitment to study Coach Rice's techniques, I'll be so much more focused, ready to take on the world, and happier because of it.

— Angela Dobson

The total person program has and will continue to be extremely beneficial during the remainder of my college years and beyond. At the beginning of the course, Coach Rice said that these lessons were the kind that you can take with you for life. Having gone through the program and used the book, I can definitely affirm this. The content of the program was an excellent combination of important life skills and topics. This will be something that I take with me for years to come, and I hope to pass it along to others. I am a definite believer and proponent of the attitude technique and total person program. I have seen the effect that it has had on me in just three months, and I am so excited to see what the long-term results will be.

— Ryan McFerrin

Wow! What can I say about such an incredible class? Leadership Fitness is the one class that I have looked forward to every week. Throughout the course, I learned about setting goals, being a positive leader, the attitude technique, financial planning, encouraging and motivating others, and the list goes on and on. I cannot wait to go through my notebook and all other materials over the holidays and organize them so I can quickly reference all of the valuable information I have received over the past several months.

— Catherine Covington

There were so many beneficial aspects of this class, but there are three lessons that have had a particularly strong impact on me: the importance of planning and writing down life goals and objectives, the impact of a positive attitude, and the best ways to interact and lead others in a beneficial way. As a result of this class, I feel truly empowered to shape my future and achieve whatever I set out to do. Also, I recently had a friend compliment me on how positive I have been acting lately and how impressed she was by my upbeat attitude. It means a lot to me to see that other people are noticing my outlook. In my positions on campus, I have been much more conscious of the type of leader that I am, and I really think that I have been a more effective and encouraging leader.

– Suzannah Gill

After taking Coach Rice's Leadership Fitness class last year and serving as his teaching assistant this year, I have witnessed the true impact of the Leadership Fitness techniques over time. When these techniques are followed, people can positively change their own lives and the lives of those around them. Coach Rice is a true friend of Georgia Tech, and through his efforts to spread the Leadership Fitness techniques, his gifts will continue to impact our society forever.

– Lauren Weatherly

I can think of no greater testament to the power of this program to change your life than what these students have written. I hope this has been, or will be, your experience, too.

Homer Rice, 2004

APPENDIX A

LEADERS FOR FREEDOM:
THE SACRIFICES OTHERS MAKE FOR US

Thoughts by Albert "Bud" Parker and Monique Gupta

In 1971, Albert "Bud" Parker married his wife, Robin Rae, and became son-in-law to her father, who was 56 years young. Bud and his father-in-law became tennis partners whenever their families came together in Birmingham, Alabama.

"I had never focused on the fact that he participated in World War II until by accident I came across his Purple Heart and the Distinguished Service Cross awarded to him by Gen. Omar Bradley," said Bud. The DSC had been earned during the early days of the invasion of Europe in June of 1944, and the Purple Heart had come from action in the Ardennes during the Battle of the Bulge.

Capt. Robert D. "Bob" Rae was a member of the 507th parachute Infantry Regiment that had been assigned to the 82nd Airborne Division for the night drop in the early hours of D-Day. As fate would have it, he was given the assignment to launch an almost suicidal assault across a fully exposed causeway that was more than 500 yards long. He was charged with securing the other side of the causeway, which was vitally important to ensure that the troops from the beach could come rapidly inland. Without hesitation, he led his men across, at a great loss of personnel, and accomplished their mission.

In a phone conversation with Gen. James Gain, who had been commanding officer at the time of the battle, Bud learned firsthand of the general's great respect for his father-in-law, and to appreciate even more what he had been willing to sacrifice that day. "I was, and have continued to be, humbled by his and his fellow veterans' sense of duty and devotion to their unit and country. Having walked the La Fiere Causeway, I am convinced it is a miracle that he made it across without being killed," said Bud. "I am glad he did, though, or I would never have met his daughter."

From that background, Bud did not hesitate to honor Bob Rae's request when, in the fall of 2000, he asked for assistance in raising funds to construct and dedicate a memorial in Normandy to the 507 PIR veterans. The unit had taken heavy casualties in securing every objective assigned to it. After Normandy, it was reassigned to the 17th Airborne Division, and after the war ended the unit was disbanded. As a result, histories of D-Day make little mention of the fact that the 507 PIR had ever been to Normandy, much less fought there. The memorial would help correct that historical oversight. The memorial's location and design were agreed upon and funds secured for the project.

On July 23, 2001, in Amfreville, France, the U.S. ambassador dedicated the memorial. Filmmaker David Druckenmiller, who had once worked at Georgia Tech, was commissioned along with Phil Walker to document the video as a gift from Bud's family to Bob and his veteran friends. The resulting film became their gift to us and all Americans, as well.

The film proved so compelling that PBS arranged to show it nationally in primetime in June 2004 during a television tribute to the 60th anniversary of D-Day. Millions rather than hundreds will now be familiar with the 507 PIR and profit from the message of their sacrifices.

"As a youngster, I was advised never to judge men by their balance sheets or their headlines, but instead by how their lives have benefited others. Over the past months, I have gained an even greater respect for not only the men of the 507 but also for all who have gone into harm's way to ensure that I have the opportunities I have had. I salute them every day," explained Bud.

He appreciated most those who were willing to volunteer to be there so that he and others could be here today, enjoying precious freedoms and opportunities that are the envy of the world. Will the rest of us and the generations to follow always remember that rich heritage and resist becoming apathetic to the lessons of history? Bud hopes so. He hopes we all will never fail to be grateful for the blessings we've inherited. By just being born in America, we have won the lottery.

"We must never forget one of the significant lessons of history," concluded Bud. "No great nation has ever endured forever. Hopefully, I, along with a growing number of Americans, will come to appreciate how very valuable and precious our citizenship in the United States of America truly is. And hopefully it will be many generations before America ceases to be the great nation it is."

The members of the 507th were truly successful positive leaders. They made it possible for each of us to have abundant opportunities now and in the future in this country.

~

Monique Gupta, a member of the Leadership Fitness class, also expressed her thoughts about patriotism. When first asked about the subject, she did not know how to respond. She is proud to be an American citizen, but she had not given much thought to the fact. The right to live in America was something she appreciated but often took for granted, she said. Her parents had had the foresight to move from India to the United States to allow her to have freedoms not possible elsewhere. They voluntarily left their families and moved across oceans to provide the best for their children. They chose a magnificent nation, one filled with opportunities, hope, and freedom.

Freedom does not always come cheaply. The documentary "D-Day: Down to Earth" reminded her of the millions of people who sacrificed so that she could feel safe and experience independence. Because of other people, today she enjoys the freedom to voice her opinions, the freedom to gain an education, and the freedom to truly live. She is thankful for the independence that no others in the world share.

"The willingness of Americans to help others always amazes me," said Monique. Americans are willing to stand up to evil and at times to sacrifice themselves for a cause greater than the individual. It is because of this unselfishness that many people across the world enjoy some rights as simple as shelter and food. America's generosity has no borders and is experienced around the world.

"I wonder how I am as lucky as I am to have earned the good fortune of being an American. The answer is, of course, that I didn't earn it. America's soldiers, their heroes, earned this for me," she wrote. "I may never be able to repay America's heroes. However, I mean to live a good life and to never forget that I was given an opportunity that so many others have not been given. I will probably never be a soldier, never sleep in a trench, never be truly afraid or alone – all of the things that others have been. But I will remembers the ones who did those things for me."

APPENDIX B

LEADERSHIP DEVELOPMENT—
THE ODK® WAY

By John D. Morgan, Executive Director
of the Omicron Delta Kappa Society, Inc.

Omicron Delta Kappa was established in 1914 at Washington and Lee University in Lexington, Virginia. Beginning as a means to recognize leaders from all phases of the campus, including faculty and administrators as well as students, the organization provides an opportunity for these individuals to collaborate for the improvement of the campus and community. Begun at a men's college, it became fully coeducational in 1974. ODK® was the first collegiate honor society of a national scope to accord recognition and honor for meritorious leadership and service in extracurricular activities and to encourage the development of general campus citizenship. It has become abundantly clear that ODK® has proved to be beneficial to many colleges and universities. Growing to more than 285 chapters is testament to the value that colleges and universities have placed and are placing on the development of citizen leaders.

A number of college curriculums have stressed the study and the development of leaders for many years. In more recent years, the specific focus of a curriculum on leadership has occurred. One of the earliest and arguably the best examples of this attention to leadership was the establishment of the Jepson School of Leadership Studies at the University of Richmond. Other schools have followed with the opportunity to complete a major or minor in leadership studies.

Leadership itself is a worthy subject of study. As has been demonstrated with the proliferation of chapters of ODK®, student leadership is worth recognizing in a special way. How does Omicron Delta Kappa define "leadership"? Does ODK® attempt to describe a particular type of leader? The answer is "yes." Those chosen to become members of this society have exhibited leadership, not only by achieving positions of leadership but also, and importantly, by behaving as leaders. This special kind of leadership occurs as leaders collaborate with others—both other students from different parts of the campus as well as faculty—with the aim of continually working together to improve their campus and community. It has its roots in ethically sound character recognition and enhancement.

While not all are selected, the honor of becoming a member of this prestigious organization is a reflection of one's integrity and perspective. Members are students of honor as well as honor students. Perhaps one of the most integral parts of this kind of leadership development is the understanding that one can always learn more, grow more, and become more.

The Omicron Delta Kappa Society, Inc., *The National Leadership Honor Society* for college students, recognizes and encourages superior scholarship, leadership and exemplary character. Membership in Omicron Delta Kappa is a mark of highest distinction and honor.

Appendix C

SPIRITUAL IMPACT/GROWTH AND DIFFERENCE THAT THE FELLOWSHIP OF CHRISTIAN ATHLETES MAKES IN LIFE

By Dal Shealy
President, Fellowship of Christian Athletes

Dr. Billy Graham once said, "A coach will impact more people in one year than the average person will in an entire lifetime."

A major corporation did a study and found that 97 percent of all the people in the world are influenced in some manner by sports. In our sports-minded world today, athletes and coaches have greater influence (along with entertainers) than most parents and teachers. They are role models, good or bad, whether they realize it – or want to be – or not.

FCA was founded in 1954 to train, equip, and encourage Christian athletes and coaches to use their platform of sports as a vehicle to share their faith. In 1956, the first FCA Camp was held at the YMCA of the Rockies in Estes Park, Colorado, with 256 athletes and coaches attending. Dr. Louis Evans, Sr., (Chaplain of the U.S. Senate) was the chaplain for the week; Branch Rickey (General Manager, Pittsburgh Pirates) spoke about signing Jackie Robinson as the first black athlete in the modern era of major league baseball (1947 with the Brooklyn Dodgers).

Outstanding professional and college athletes and coaches were fed spiritually, mentally and physically for a week. Thus, FCA was launched full-speed with its mission: "To present to athletes and coaches, and all whom they influence, the challenge and adventure of receiving Jesus Christ as Savior and Lord, serving Him in their relationships and in the fellowships of the church."

Does FCA make a difference in life? Does FCA have a spiritual, physical and/or mental impact? Does it help growth in performance, inspiration or motivation, as it demonstrates a whole-life transformation through Christ in sports?

During 2003, we experienced too many tragic situations with high-profile coaches and athletes. Improper conduct, drinking, and fraternizing, murder of a player, attempted cover-ups, misuse of school credit cards, stealing, gaming, etc. So, how successful is FCA in making a difference on and off the field or arena of competition?

On nearly 10,000 campuses across the country, around 300,000 students are being led in Bible studies and small group discussions, learning how to live their lives for Christ. As a sports-based ministry, FCA is teaching them how to compete for an "audience of One."

Let's look at the reasons behind the success.

TEAM FCA: TEAM FCA is made up of athletes and coaches (and everyone they influence) who seek to compete for Christ. Beginning in the fall of 2003, competitors officially can become part of TEAM FCA by signing the Competitor's Creed:

THE COMPETITOR'S CREED

I am a Christian first and last.
I am created in the likeness of God Almighty to bring Him glory.
I am a member of Team Jesus Christ.
I wear the colors of the cross.

I am a Competitor now and forever.
I am made to strive, to strain, to stretch and to succeed in the
    arena of competition.
I am a Christian Competitor and as such, I face my challenger
    with the face of Christ.

I do not trust in myself.
I do not boast in my abilities or believe in my own strength.
I rely solely on the power of God.
I compete for the pleasure of my Heavenly Father, the honor of
    Christ and the reputation of the Holy Spirit.

My attitude on and off the field is above reproach—my conduct
    beyond criticism.
Whether I am preparing, practicing or playing;
I submit to God's authority and those He has put over me.
I respect my coaches, officials, teammates and competitors out
    of respect for the Lord.

My body is the temple of Jesus Christ.
I protect it from within and without.
Nothing enters my body that does not honor the Living God.
My sweat is an offering to my Master. My soreness is a sacrifice
    to my Savior.

I give my all—all of the time.

I do not give up. I do not give in. I do not give out.
I am the Lord's warrior—a competitor by conviction and a disciple
    of determination.
I am confident beyond reason because my confidence lies in Christ.
The result of my efforts must result in His glory.

Let the competition begin.
Let the glory be God's

FCA seeks to develop competitors for Christ through leadership
training with the values of Integrity, Serving, Teamwork and
Excellence:

Integrity. . . We will demonstrate Christ-like wholeness, privately
    and publicly.

Serving. . . We will model Jesus' example of serving.

Teamwork. . . We will express our unity in Christ.

Excellence. . . We will honor and glorify God in all we do.

Many times a person will read the sports page or a sport magazine, but they will not read the Bible. They will go to an athletic contest before they go to church. Our desired goal is to produce and mentor athletes and coaches to join TEAM FCA and
live and play by The Competitor's Creed.

   Christian coaches must understand that they may be the only
Bible their athletes read, and their game may be the only church
folks attend. Their influence in and outside the arena can and
will have a very positive impact on FCA's vision: "To see the
world impacted for Jesus Christ through the influence of athletes
and coaches."

FCA is broken down into the 4C's of ministry:

Coaches Ministry —At the heart of FCA are coaches. Our role is to minister to them by encouraging and equipping them to know and serve Christ. FCA ministers to coaches through Bible studies, staff contacts, prayer support, discipleship and mentoring, resources, outreach events, national and local conventions, conferences, and retreats.

Campus Ministries —The Campus Ministry is initiated and led by student-athletes and coaches on junior high, high school and college campuses. The programs of the Campus ministry include Huddles, Team Bible Studies, Chapel Program, Team FCA Membership, *One Way 2 Play — Drug Free!* * and Special Events.

Camps Ministry —Camps are a time of "inspiration and perspiration" for athletes and coaches to reach their potential by offering comprehensive athletic, spiritual and leadership training. The types of Camps are Sports Camp, Leadership Camp, Coaches Camp, Youth Sports Camp and Partnership Camp.

Community Ministry —The non-school based FCA ministries reach the community through partnerships with the local churches, businesses, parents and volunteers. These ministries not only reach out to the community but also allow the community to invest in athletes and coaches. Community Ministries include Stewardship Ministries, Adult Ministries, Sport-Specific Ministries, Membership, Urban Initiatives, Global Sports Development, Clinics, Product and Resource Development, and Professional Athlete Ministries.

*The *One Way 2 Play — Drug Free!* Program is the only one of its kind. It is based on Faith, Commitment (signed card) and Accountability, where an individual meets with another person on a weekly basis to give account of his/her actions during the past week.

In a survey of the FCA OW2P! program, written by the George Gallup organization and executed by Public and Private Venture, the effort was found to be 81percent successful. The athletes and coaches who signed abstained from drugs, alcohol, steroids, and tobacco.

Another section of the survey asked the following question: Who or what influenced you to sign the OW2P! commitment card?

28 percent said that it was their coach.
22 percent said it was an FCA teammate.
19 percent said it was their belief in God.
12 percent said it was fear of becoming addicted.
10 percent said it was a speaker at a FCA event.
Only 7 percent said it was (a) parent(s).

Another way to look at it is that nearly 70 percent said it was either something with their relationship with the Lord and/or their sport – the two things that define FCA.

TEAM FCA members also are taught:
- use of weapons and acts of violence are not the way to solve personal problems;
- to promote healing of relationships and reconciliation among peers;
- to honor all life, born and unborn; and
- to treat each other with respect and dignity.

When athletes and coaches make a faith commitment to be all God created and gifted them to be, and to be a disciple (follower) of Jesus Christ, they strive to take out of their lives the things that cause them to stumble and fall. Many of those who are failing get noticed publicity and give the 95 percent who are striving to be their best a difficult task in the public eye.

APPENDIX D

NUTRITION

By Chris Rosenbloom, Ph.D., R.D.
Associate Dean, College of Health and Human Sciences
Associate Professor, Department of Nutrition
Georgia State University, Atlanta, Georgia

The Atlanta Journal-Constitution publishes a column called "The Vent," where people write or call the paper and "vent." My favorite vent was, "If you are what you eat, then I'm fast, cheap, and easy." Too many Americans fall into the fast, cheap, and easy category. In fact, most Americans probably give more thought to choosing gas for their cars or food for their pets than they do for themselves.

What does nutrition have to do with leadership? As you read the pages of this book, you learned that leaders need to attend to their physical, mental, and spiritual well-being. Good nutrition is a big part of physical and mental well-being. Without proper fuel, in the form of food and fluids, the brain is not as effective or efficient and the body will lack energy. People are always saying they need more energy; the best way to get more energy is to start with your food habits.

My five tips for a healthy body are:

1. Eat breakfast every day. Breakfast does what it says — it breaks the fast. People who eat breakfast get more nutrients during the day than breakfast skippers. Breakfast eaters have more energy to get through their morning activities and are less hungry when lunchtime rolls around. And, for those of you still in school, breakfast eaters score better on exams. Breakfast supplies your body with needed glucose and your brain prefers glucose as a fuel. What is a "good" breakfast?

Any combination of whole grain carbohydrates and protein makes a healthy breakfast. Some examples are:

- Pumpernickel bagel with peanut butter

- Whole grain toast with a slice of cheddar cheese

- High fiber breakfast cereal with low fat milk

- Fruit-flavored yogurt topped with chopped nuts

- Scrambled egg rolled in a whole-wheat tortilla

2. Choose a colorful diet. Nature provided foods with a rainbow of colors for a reason. The colorful pigments in foods help protect foods against diseases, and when we eat plants we are afforded some of that protection. Choose a diet with a wide variety of colors, as these foods have been shown to be protective against the two most prevalent diseases of Americans: heart disease and cancer. When choosing foods, go for the most colorful ones you can find. For example:

- Select pink grapefruit.

- Toss blueberries on your cereal.

- Snack on frozen red grapes.

- Bake a sweet potato instead of a white potato.

- Make trail mix with whole-grain cereal and dried cranberries.

- Eat dried apricots and peaches instead of cookies after a meal.

- Sprinkle low-fat frozen yogurt with fresh or frozen raspberries.

- Choose dark green leafy salad greens over iceberg lettuce.

- Top your salad with bell peppers, cucumber slices, and tomatoes.

- Try spinach, mushrooms, and green peppers on pizza.

3. Be savvy about healthful fats. Fats are an important part of the diet, but not all fats are created equal. Solid fats, such as butter, stick margarine, hydrogenated fats, and animal fats found in whole milk, cream, cheese, and meat, are high in saturated fat and can raise blood cholesterol levels. Softer or liquid fats are better choices. The best choices are olive oil, canola oil, safflower oil, or soft-tub margarines. All fats have the same amount of calories, even though their effects on blood cholesterol differ, so even the "good" fats should be kept to moderate portions. Suggestions for eating more healthy fats are:

- Read labels to uncover hidden hydrogenated fats.

- Use olive oil and flavored vinegar to toss your salad.

- Switch to light or non-fat versions of cream cheese, mayonnaise, and sour cream.

- Learn to enjoy grilled, baked, or broiled meats instead of fried meats.

- Say no to fried appetizers like mozzarella sticks, jalapeno peppers, and fried vegetables.

- Sautee vegetables in olive oil and add to cooked pasta.

- Put a slice of avocado on your sandwich instead of a high fat spread like mayonnaise.

4. Eat whole grains, fruits, and vegetables for quality carbohydrates. People perceive that carbohydrates are "bad" and protein is "good." The truth is that both nutrients are important for good health and to fuel an active lifestyle. Make the switch to quality carbohydrates – those carbohydrate-rich foods that provide fibers, vitamins, and minerals. Whole-grain breads, cereals, pasta, rice, fresh or frozen vegetables and whole fruits all contain quality carbs.

- Choose breads that contain whole-wheat flour as the first ingredient.

- Don't be fooled by the word "wheat" bread – only whole wheat has fiber.

- Try brown rice instead of white rice.

- Choose whole grain pastas over refined white pasta.

- Select whole fruit more often than fruit juice.

- Pick fresh fruits in season; when out of season, try frozen fruit without added sugar.

- Check out the wide variety of washed and sliced fresh vegetables and fruits in the grocery store produce section.

- Pumpernickel bagels are a good alternative to wheat bagels.

5. Work activity into your life to prevent weight creep. Growing old and gaining weight don't have to go hand-in-hand, but you have to work hard to prevent it. People who are active not only keep their weight in check, but they decrease their risk for high blood pressure, heart disease, colon cancer, and osteoporosis. Active people have positive mental outlooks and suffer form less depression than sedentary people. As we age, we lose muscle and gain fat. Try to work as much activity into your daily life as possible to help avoid weight creep.

- Start a weight-training program to preserve muscle mass – use free weights or weight machines to keep and build muscle.

- Run with your dog; play touch football with your kids, or go for family bicycle rides.

- Walk around the block after dinner instead of watching television.

- When shopping, make frequent trips to your car with pac ages and walk around the mall a few times before making your first purchase.

- Use the "five and ten" rule for stairs – walk up if it is five flights or fewer and walk down if it is 10 flights of stairs or fewer.

- Buy a pedometer and measure your steps – aim for 10,000 steps a day

By making these small changes in your diet, you can have more energy, reduce your risk or chronic disease and avoid weight gain. And remember: It's never too late to start!

APPENDIX E

THE CASE FOR NUTRITIONAL SUPPLEMENTATION

By J. Alexander Bralley, Ph.D.
CEO – Metametrix Clinical Laboratory

For many years, nutrition scientists have said that Americans can get all their nutritional needs from eating a good diet. Supplementation of vitamins and minerals was not necessary and simply created "expensive urine." More recently, this conventional wisdom is being challenged as evidence accumulates on the benefits of supplementation.

It is really quite difficult, as it turns out, for people to eat a healthy diet with the use of fast foods and/or the highly processed foods common in the standard American diet. It is very easy to eat a lot of calories but these calories are, more often than not, empty calories – high in fat and carbohydrates but very low in essential nutrients like vitamins and minerals.

In an article published in the prestigious *New England Journal of Medicine* in 2001, Dr Walter Willett, chairman of the Nutrition and Epidemiology Department at Harvard's School of Public Health, argued that individuals need to start taking supplemental nutrients to help maintain optimal wellness. He also pointed out that the risk of chronic disease was significantly decreased in those who did. [1] This groundbreaking article set the stage for greater understanding and general acceptance of the great health value that regular supplementation can provide. In the same light, Dr. Bruce Ames, noted cancer researcher at UC Berkeley, has published several articles indicating vitamin, mineral and anti-oxidant supplementation can decrease cancer risk and slow aging of the brain. [2, 3]

What do essential nutrients do? Why are they so vital to the maintenance of good health and prevention of disease? Vitamins and minerals are called essential nutrients because the body cannot make them. They must, therefore, be consumed in the diet. So if one is eating a junk-food diet with low nutrient content or if one has increased demands for certain nutrients, it is relatively easy to develop nutrient deficiencies which can adversely affect health.

Vitamins are also called coenzymes and minerals are called cofactors. They function in the body to assist in the conversion of one compound into another. Special proteins called enzymes perform this task. All the functions of the human body boil down to the ability of these enzymes to work properly. If a cofactor or coenzyme is not present in the appropriate amounts, the enzyme does not work as it should and a dysfunction can occur. About 22 percent of all enzymes in the body require a coenzyme or vitamin to work properly. Many enzymes also require mineral cofactors to work. More than 300 enzymes, for example, use zinc, yet the body needs only about 10 mg. per day of zinc before a deficiency develops.

While the classic deficiency diseases such as pellagra, beri beri, rickets, etc., rarely exist in developed countries like the U.S., the work of researchers like Drs. Willett and Ames is showing the health benefits of essential nutrient adequacy. I refer to this situation as avoiding the development of nutrient deficiencies. That is, one may not be so deficient in a nutrient to cause a classic deficiency disease, but one still might be in a situation where enough of the nutrient is not present to adequately allow the enzyme to function optimally. Dr. Ames recently published a paper illustrating this point using genetic diseases as a model of how nutrients can prevent disease. [4] In this paper he points out that many disease processes may benefit from nutrient supplementation in higher doses than the RDA amounts, particularly the anti-oxidants such as vitamin E, C and lipoic acid.

So if you eat the standard American diet, are over or under weight, under stress, are still growing, pregnant, nursing, sick or have been sick recently, participate in sports, don't get enough sleep, smoke, or any of the above, you would do well to be taking at least a good quality vitamin and mineral formula with additional anti-oxidants. Everyone is different, and what may be adequate for one person may not be sufficient for another. This situation can be caused by either the unique genetics of the person or increased needs for a particular nutrient.

A more recent trend has been to actually test a person for unique nutritional needs. Metametrix has had 20 years of experience in this area. Laboratory testing at Metametrix allows one to design custom nutrient formulations for all types of people, ranging from those with chronic illnesses to high-performance, professional athletes. It has always been interesting for me to see the diversity of nutrient needs in the population. Children in particular are in need for supplementing their diets, which in most cases, in my experience, are of exceedingly poor quality. Good nutrition at this age is important for several reasons. Chronic illnesses of aging really begin when we are young. Prevention pays off early. Also, I feel the dramatic increase in behavioral disorders in children is due to poor nutrition that dramatically affects brain function.

The bottom line is this: Do you and your family a favor and

invest in a quality nutritional supplement program for a happy and healthy future.

SOURCES:

1. Willett, W.C. and M.J. Stampfer, *Clinical practice. What vitamins should I be taking, doctor?* N Engl J Med, 2001. 345(25): p. 1819-24.

2. Ames, B.N. and P. Wakimoto, *Are vitamin and mineral deficiencies a major cancer risk?* Nat Rev Cancer, 2002. 2(9): p. 694-704.

3. Liu, J., et al., *Delaying brain mitochondrial decay and aging with mitochondrial antioxidants and metabolites.* Ann N Y Acad Sci, 2002. 959: p. 133-66.

4. Ames, B.N., I. Elson-Schwab, and E.A. Silver, *High-dose vitamin therapy stimulates variant enzymes with decreased coenzyme binding affinity (increased K(m)): relevance to genetic disease and polymorphisms.* Am J Clin Nutr, 2002. 75(4): p. 616-58.

APPENDIX F

HOW TO BE A SURVIVOR: GUIDELINES ON LIVING WELL TO AGE 100

By John D. Cantwell, M.D.
Cardiology of Georgia, P.C. Medical Director of the
Homer Rice Medical Clinic, Georgia Tech

Let's begin with the opposite approach. If you wish to shorten your life, or to make your so-called "golden years" more miserable, there are several things you can do. Heading the list is to smoke cigarettes. This can make you a prime candidate for an early heart attack, often fatal. It can appreciably increase your risk of lung cancer, and multiple other types of cancers (mouth, esophagus, stomach, pancreas, uterine, cervix, colon, bladder, and kidney). Cigarettes are also a major cause of chronic disabling lung diseases such as emphysema.

Eating too much and exercising too little leads to diseases such as obesity and diabetes, both in epidemic proportions. These disorders can accelerate cardiovascular disease and contribute to kidney failure, heart failure, blindness, and loss of an extremity.

Don't pay any attention to your blood pressure level, and eat all the salt and fast foods you desire. This can increase your chance of developing a stroke, with the disability that so frequently accompanies it. Over the years uncontrolled hypertension can also damage the kidneys and lead to heart attacks and heart failure.

The same applies to ignoring your blood cholesterol level. This easily treated disorder, if elevated, can facilitate the premature onset of coronary heart disease, peripheral vascular disease, and strokes.

Binge alcohol drinking is another good way to shorten your life, especially if coupled with reckless driving, preferably without a seat belt. Heavy alcohol use (a steady dose of more than two standard-sized drinks daily) can over a period of years damage the liver and the heart muscle. It can also contribute to interpersonal woes and marital discord.

A disregard for feelings of depression can add to the misery of life by creating an "inability to experience pleasure" and can be a risk factor for suicide, the third leading cause of death in young people.

ASSESSING YOUR HEALTH STATUS

As Henry David Thoreau once wrote, "Every man is the building of a temple, called his body.... We are all sculptors and painters, and our material is our own flesh and blood and bones."

What kind of temple are you building? Let's take an inventory of your health status by answering the following 10 questions:

1. Using Figure 1 (on page 197), calculate your body mass index (BMI), based on your height and weight. Your BMI is _____, placing you in the

normal   overweight   obese

(circle one) category.

2. List the average number of aerobic-exercise minutes you get each day.

_____ None
_____ 5-10
_____ 10-30
_____30-60
_____over 60

3. Do you smoke? _____ Yes _____ No If yes, _____ packs per day.

4. Get a blood test to learn your total cholesterol _____ and your HDL cholesterol _____ levels.

5. Measure your waist circumference (_____ inches).

6. Fill out the depression questionnaire (Figure 2, on page 198).

7. List your average weekly alcohol intake:
_____beers _____1½ oz. hard liquor _____4oz. glasses of wine

8. Check your own blood pressure at a drug store, grocery store, or fire station: _____ mmHg.

9. Indicate if you almost always wear seatbelts in a car:
_____ Yes _____ No

10. Review your family history.
Any men with heart attacks before age 55?
_____ Yes _____ No
Any women with heart attacks before age 65?
_____ Yes _____ No

Any sudden, unexplained deaths?
_____ Yes _____ No
Any relatives with depression?
_____ Yes _____ No

PUTTING PREVENTIVE MEDICINE INTO PRACTICE

The foundation of a good preventive medicine program is daily
exercise and a sound diet. Current guidelines recommend 30-60
minutes of endurance exercise most days (brisk walking, jogging, cycling, rowing, swimming, aerobics, etc.). Weight training
at least three times a week is advised, along with regular stretch-
ing exercises. Men over age 40 or women 50 or above with certain coronary risk factors (hypertension, elevated cholesterol
level, prior cigarettes, family history of heart attacks) should
consider an exercise test before beginning a program more stren-
uous than just walking.

A Mediterranean-type diet seems prudent, emphasizing fish,
vegetables, fruit, nuts, and lean meat, reducing the dietary
calories enough to achieve a normal body mass index. The
Ornish and Pritikin diets work for a few but are too rigid for
most. The Atkins diet and other low-carbohydrate programs
are somewhat controversial and don't seem the answer to long-
term weight management.

Alcohol can be used in moderation – no more than two standard-sized drinks per day for men and one for women (who
don't metabolize alcohol as well as men). Those with a family
history of alcoholism, or with inability to moderate their own
alcohol intake, had best abstain. Red wine is hyped in the media,
but most studies suggest equal health benefits from beer, wine,
or hard liquor.

The ideal blood pressure is less than or equal to 120/80

mmHg. Those with readings between 120-139/80-89 are now considered to be "pre-hypertensive". A diagnosis of hypertension is made when readings average 140/90 or above.

Non-drug ways to control blood pressure include exercise, weight loss if overweight, reductions in dietary salt and stress, and increases in dietary potassium. When the blood pressure remains above 140/90 mmHg despite therapeutic lifestyle changes, a variety of very effective medications are now available. For young, athletic people with hypertension, I generally start with a drug that blocks the angiotensin-converting enzyme (ACE), leading to muscle relaxation and dilation in the arteries. Angiotensin-receptor blockers (ARBs) work in a similar fashion. For others, I'll use a low dose of a diuretic, a beta-blocker drug (that reduces the adrenaline effect in the arteries) or, infrequently, several medicines are combined to achieve a normal blood pressure.

Patients with hypertension are encouraged to monitor their own blood pressure, using a simple digital home blood pressure monitor, and to record the results on graph paper.

When the blood LDL (low-density lipoprotein) cholesterol level exceeds 100 mg/dl, dietary cholesterol should be decreased to less than 300 mg daily, and saturated fat to less than 10 grams daily. Take Control and Benecol can be used in place of butter or margarine, as they help reduce cholesterol absorption from the intestine.

For those with LDL cholesterol levels still above 160 mg/dl, despite dietary efforts, effective drugs are available to achieve the desired goal. So-called "statin" drugs (like Lipitor, Zocor, Pravachol, etc.) can be tried in tiny doses, like 5 to 10mg, three times a week. Those drugs block an enzyme in the liver that is involved in the manufacture of cholesterol. Other effective drugs include fibrates (Tricor, Lopid) and the B vitamin, niacin.

TWENTY-FIVE GUIDELINES ON LIVING WELL TO AGE 100

1. Keep the body mass index well below 25 by eating less and exercising more.

2. Try to do at least 30-60 minutes of endurance exercise (fast walking, jogging, cycling, swimming, aerobics, etc.) most days.

3. Stay mentally active. Keep busy. Learn new things.

4. Avoid hardening of the arteries (atherosclerosis). Keep the total cholesterol under 200 mg/dl, ideally under 180 mg/dl. Strive for a HDL level well above 40 mg/dl, a triglyceride level below 150 mg/dl, an LDL cholesterol level at least under 100 mg/dl and preferably below 80 mg/dl.

5. Take a buffered 81 mg aspirin table at least every other day, beginning at age 25. Also take a multivitamin that contains at least 400 mcg of folic acid.

6. Women should get regular Pap smears beginning at age 30, and yearly mammograms starting at age 40.

7. Prostate cancer screening, with the PSA blood test, should be done at ages 40, 44, 48, and then yearly beginning at age 50.

8. A colonoscopy test to screen for pre-cancerous polyps is advised at least every 10 years for men and women, starting at age 50. Those with polyps may need more frequent follow-up exams.

9. Do bone density tests to screen for osteoporosis, every 10 years beginning at age 60, for men and women.

10. Preserve your hearing by avoiding exposure to loud noises (above 75 decibels).

11. Live close to your children and grandchildren in later years, if possible.

12. Don't smoke, and avoid oral tobacco and second-hand smoke.

13. Avoid trans fatty acids (in fast foods and a lot of baked goods). Read labels on food to assess trans fat and saturated fat content.

14. Wear seat belts in motor vehicles. Drive defensively. Don't drink alcohol and drive.

15. Limit daily alcohol to an average of less than or equal to two standard-sized drinks for men, one for women. Go some days without any. If you have a family history of alcoholism, or have difficulty using alcohol in moderation, avoid it completely.

16. Get regular check ups, especially when you reach age 35, to include at least a brief office visit, rectal exam, stool test for occult blood, and blood cholesterol and HDL measurement.

17. Get adequate sleep.

18. Have your home checked for radon and asbestos.

19. Avoid small airplanes whenever possible.

20. Minimize sun exposure. Use sunscreen and wear hats.

21. Avoid anxiety-producing situations as much as you can. If prone to depression, get medical help early and take suicide precautions.

22. Know your blood fat, blood sugar, and blood pressure numbers. Strive for a blood pressure at least under 130/80 mmHg (under 120/80 mmHg is ideal) and a blood sugar below 110 mg/dl.

23. Try to drink up to eight glasses of water daily.

24. Simplify your life. It is a curious paradox that "finding a way to live the simple life is one of today's most complicated problems."

25. Develop a spiritual base. Do things for others and focus less on your own wants.

REFERENCES

1. Perls, T.T. and Silver, M.H. *Living to 100.* Basic Books, New York, 1999.

2. Yahn, G. "The Impact of Holistic Medicine, Medical Groups and Health Concepts," *JAMA* 1979; 242: 2202-2205.

Figure 1: Body Mass Index (BMI chart).
Figure 2: Zung Self-Rating Depression Scale.

FIGURE 1
WEIGHT YOUR RISK WITH BMI

How to use this chart:

1. Look down the left column to find your height.
2. Look across that row and find the weight nearest your own.
3. Look to the number at the top of the column to identify your BMI.
4. If your number is 27 or greater, you may be at risk.

BODY MASS INDEX CHART

Body Weight (pounds)

Height (inches)	19	20	21	22	23	24	25	26	27	28	29	30	31	32	33	34	35
58	91	96	100	105	110	115	119	124	129	134	138	143	148	153	158	162	167
59	94	99	104	109	114	119	124	128	133	138	143	148	153	158	163	168	173
60	97	102	107	112	118	123	128	133	138	143	148	153	158	163	168	174	179
61	100	106	111	116	122	127	132	137	143	148	153	158	164	169	174	180	185
62	104	109	115	120	126	131	136	142	147	153	158	164	169	175	180	186	191
63	107	113	118	124	130	135	141	146	152	158	163	169	175	180	186	191	197
64	110	116	122	128	134	140	145	151	157	163	169	174	180	186	192	197	204
65	114	120	126	132	138	144	150	156	162	168	174	180	186	192	198	204	210
66	118	124	130	136	142	148	155	161	167	173	179	186	192	198	204	210	216
67	121	127	134	140	146	153	159	166	172	178	185	191	198	204	211	217	223
68	125	131	138	144	151	158	164	171	177	184	190	197	203	210	216	223	230
69	128	135	142	149	155	162	169	176	182	189	196	203	209	216	223	230	236
70	132	139	146	153	160	167	174	181	188	195	202	209	216	222	229	236	243
71	136	143	150	157	165	172	179	186	193	200	208	215	222	229	236	243	250
72	140	147	154	162	169	177	184	191	199	206	213	221	228	235	242	250	258
73	144	151	159	166	174	182	189	197	204	212	219	227	235	242	250	257	265
74	148	155	163	171	179	186	194	202	210	218	225	233	241	249	256	264	272
75	152	160	168	176	184	192	200	208	216	224	232	240	248	256	264	272	279
76	156	164	172	180	189	197	205	213	221	230	238	246	254	263	271	279	287

Source: National Heart, Lung, and Blood Institute.

MEASURING BODY MASS

The new body mass index (BMI) applies to both men and women. To determine BMI, weight in kilograms is divided by height in meters, squared. To calculate your body mass index from the table on page 197, locate your height in inches in the left-hand column, then follow it across until you locate your weight; the number at the very top is your body mass index. A BMI of 25 to 29.9 is considered overweight and one of 30 or above is considered obese.

FIGURE 2
ARE YOU DEPRESSED?

Answer the questions below to find out your potential for depression.

	Yes	No
1. I feel downhearted, blue, and sad.	___	___
2. I don't enjoy the things that I used to.	___	___
3. I feel others would be better off if I were dead.	___	___
4. I feel that I am not useful or needed.	___	___
5. I notice that I am losing weight.	___	___
6. I have trouble sleeping through the night.	___	___
7. I am restless and can't keep still.	___	___
8. My mind isn't as clear as it used to be.	___	___
9. I get tired for no reason.	___	___
10. I feel hopeless about the future.	___	___

If you answered "Yes" to at least five questions, and you answered "Yes" to Question 1 or Question 2, and these symptoms have persisted for at least two weeks, you may be suffering from serious depression. To find out more about how depression may be affecting you, get in touch with a mental health professional or your family physician.

If you answered "Yes" to Question 3—regardless of how you answered the other questions—you should seek help immediately.

If you suspect a loved one is depressed, give this questionnaire to him or her.

Adapted from the Zung Self-Rating Depression Scale© (William W.K. Zung, 1965, 1974, all rights reserved).

Appendix G

50 STEPS TO POSITIVE LEADERSHIP

By Hank McCamish
McCamish Group, Inc.

1. Write Your Story

Write, in a paragraph or two, the story of the future you desire. Write what you'll be doing, where you'll be living, and the successes you'll be enjoying. This will be a motivator for you in both the immediate present and the future.

2. Visualize Into the Future

Close your eyes and see yourself doing whatever it is that you wish to be doing. If you want to get in shape, picture a slim, healthy you running or working out. If your dream is to start a small business, see yourself on opening day, greeting customers and employees.

3. Visualize Backwards

When you visualize backwards, you see where you were and how far you have come. If your goal was to get organized and you have made enormous improvement in that area, visualize back to when things weren't going so well. This will keep you heading in the right direction.

4. Dream Big
When you think about your future, don't be afraid to dream big. This will make short-term failures easier to handle. When you hit an obstacle, it won't stop you because your eyes are set on a bigger goal.

5. Educate Yourself
Learn, read, talk about, listen, and experience everything you can about your particular goal or dream. If you wish to be an author, you can take classes, read books, write, talk with other writers, join workshops, etc.

6. Get Organized
A clean, tidy, and well-organized home, office, and life is a must for the motivated mind. Physical clutter can easily lead to mental clutter. Keep your life organized, and you will find more energy and clarity in every day.

7. Place Motivators in Your Home and Office
Place symbols, signs, notes, or objects that remind you of your goals and dreams in your home, office, car, wallet, and write them into your planner or calendar. These reminders will guarantee a constant stream of motivation.

8. Volunteer
Volunteer your time to helping others. When you give of yourself, you will realize how much you have in your own life and how satisfying it is to make others happy.

9. Help Others with Motivation
Only when you teach others do you fully understand the subject at hand. Help your children to get motivated, help your friends to set effective goals, help your husband or wife to

achieve personal dreams.

10. Spend Time with Children

Spending time with children will put things in perspective for you. You may be stressed out from work and worried about getting everything done on time, but when you play with your kids, the worries and stress seem to melt away. Children have a simple way of looking at things, and that is something we could all benefit from.

11. Create a Buddy System

Do you have a close friend who is trying to accomplish something? Is your wife or husband setting goals for improvement? If so, join in a buddy system. You will each serve to motivate the other, offering words of encouragement and helpful reminders as you both progress towards your particular goals.

12. Find A Role Model

Choose a role model to learn from. You won't have to reinvent the wheel when you can follow an exemplary person you respect.

13. Take a Walk or Drive

Take a walk around the block or a short drive through the neighborhood to relax, reflect, and enjoy some quiet time. We all need a break now and then, and a quick walk or drive is the perfect solution.

14. Read Success Stories

Read the success stories of those around you. In the daily newspaper alone there are dozens of small success stories that can motivate and inspire you to action. The library is filled with autobiographies and biographies of ordinary men and women who have done extraordinary things.

15. Listen to Music

Music can calm, excite, sadden, and even motivate. Listening to the "Rocky" theme song while running is a great way to use music as a motivator. What's your motivating song?

16. Watch Motivating Movies

One reason people enjoy watching movies is because of the hero's tale. A young, unexpected hero is called to action. After struggling throughout the movie, he learns, grows, and is victorious in the end. This is motivation at its best. Make a list of movies that motivate you and build a small library to use as your motivation station.

17. Read Motivational Quotations

Located on the Internet and in books are thousands of quotations that inspire, motivate, and cause us all to think about our lives in a different way. Search the Internet for quotations, and you will find thousands of pages that match just what you are looking for.

18. Create a Healthy Diet

Energy is very important to living a happy life, but that depends upon healthy eating. Be sure to create a healthy diet that includes all of the necessary nutrients, minerals, and vitamins for your system. Following the basic food table is a good guide, for starters.

19. Get Enough Sleep

Some people can get by on six hours, while others require seven to eight. Regardless of what you need in sleep, make sure you get enough. A few nights in a row of only three or four hours will take its toll on your motivation, energy, and attitude.

20. Use Goals in Your Life

This is the most important tip about goals: use them! Without goals, you will have a difficult time improving any area of your life. Leaving your future up to chance isn't a good way to get what you want. Make use of goals throughout your life and enjoy the success and happiness they bring.

21. Brainstorm

Get out a clean sheet of paper and a pen. Sit in a quiet, well-lit area, and think, think, think. Write any ideas that pop into your head – financial goals, personal goals, relationship goals, health goals, etc. Write every idea, and when you're finished, you'll have more than enough goals to work with.

22. Write Your Goal on Paper

Once you select a goal to work towards, write it on paper. This makes it more tangible and concrete. A goal that is left to float around in your head may be forgotten before you have had a chance to work on it.

23. Make Your Goal Specific

Goals must be specific in order to be effective. Improving your relationship with your children is an important and worthwhile goal, but it may be too broad. Instead, your plan could include a play-day once a week, family dinnertime each night from 6:00 to 7:00, and a game night once a week. Such plans have a greater chance of success.

24. Use Deadlines

Procrastination is deadly to your goals and objectives. A great way to leapfrog that problem is to give your goal a deadline. As with the goal itself, make your deadline specific.

25. Use a Start Date

Deadlines are very important to goal setting, but we can't forget about their counterpart – start dates. Once a goal is created, you may have many reasons for putting it off. Give your goal a start date and stick to it.

26. Make Your Goals Challenging

In order for goals to be effective, they must be challenging. If your goal is too easy to achieve, your motivation and dedication will decrease. Your goals should make you reach and extend your current abilities and skills.

27. Make Your Goals Achievable

Setting a goal that is completely out of your reach will cause frustration, anger, and self-doubt. Be sure to set goals that challenge you but that are also reasonable.

28. Make a Detailed Plan of Action

Create a detailed, step-by-step plan of action for each part of your goal. One of the main reasons many goals are not accomplished is the lack of understanding of what needs to be done. Plan your work, and work your plan.

29. Don't Overdo It

Don't set too many goals at once. One to three is a good number to start with. Spreading yourself too thin will create a situation where no single goal will receive the attention it requires.

30. Measure Your Progress

Measure your progress as you work on your goal. You may wish to write a 300-page novel. Don't set 300 pages as the only goal. Break it up into 25- to 50-page increments and keep a daily tally of the pages you complete. Measuring your progress keeps your motivation peaking during your goal's lifecycle.

31. Wish List
Make a list of 10 things that you want to do in life – start a business, run a marathon, visit Europe, learn French, etc. Put the list in a drawer in your office or home.

32. Quick Reminders
Sticky notes are great tools to help you remember your daily tasks and goals. Just don't overdo it. You don't want so many notes stuck to your computer screen that you can't read what's on it.

33. Reward Yourself
Set a reward for yourself. If you accomplish a small step or your entire goal, celebrate. You've worked hard and you deserve it. Go out to dinner with your family, take a short vacation, or do anything else that makes you happy.

34. WIIFM?
Why are you setting this goal? Write "What's In It For Me?" for each one of your goals. You must be able to state clearly the reasons why you are setting this goal. If you cannot, delete the goal from your list and move to the next one.

35. Use the Right Words
Use statements like, "I have a positive attitude," or, "We'll find a solution," in daily conversation. The words you use on a daily basis have a major impact on your attitude and moods.

36. Strive for Optimism
I have spoken with many people who see being a pessimist or an optimist as a 50/50 chance, believing one is just as good as the

other. That is a trap! Having a positive attitude is something you should strive for. It isn't something you are or are not. It is something you can become.

37. What Company Do You Keep?
Do your friends have negative attitudes? Does it rub off on you? Many times the company we keep can affect our attitudes. If your group at work or at home negatively affects your attitude, take the necessary steps to change the situation.

38. When You Know You Need a Change
When you know you aren't happy, admit it to yourself and take action to reverse it. This is a very difficult thing to do, especially if you aren't in the mood to admit things to yourself. It may be hard, but it is worth it. When you are being negative, realize it and change it.

39. Listen to What Others Say
We may like to tell ourselves that we are positive people, but it's not always true. Listen to what your friends and family say about your attitude. They may say things that you don't want to hear, but sometimes the best changes in life come from constructive criticism.

40. Learn What Makes You Tick
When you know what makes you upset, you will be able to avoid those situations and save yourself the tension and frustration they bring. If you cannot avoid the situation, learn how to make the best of it

41. What Makes You Happy?
This is vital to your attitude and mood. Your "happy" buttons will serve to improve your attitude again and again. When I'm

not in a good mood, I first ask myself if I have eaten that day. More often than not, after getting food into my system, my attitude does a complete 180-degree turnaround.

42. Give Yourself a Break

Give yourself a quick time-out now and then when you are becoming stressed or upset. Often a short break can help you put things in perspective and return to the situation with a positive demeanor.

43. Think Twice Before You Act Once

Before you act, think about what your action will cause. If an employee does something wrong that negatively affects you, don't attack. Think about the best response. Only after you have done this twice should you take action.

44. React vs. Respond

These two words are the difference between a happy, enthusiastic, positive person and a sad, frustrated, negative person. When anything happens in life that affects you, both directly and indirectly, respond to the situation. This means you think about it, use reason to find a solution, and take appropriate measures. When you react, you skip the reasoning stage and do what comes naturally in the moment. This only causes more problems and frustrations. Respond. Do not react.

45. Appreciate the Things You Have

Look around you and learn to appreciate everything you have in your life – your friends, family, career, home, etc. This is enough to create a positive attitude because no matter how bad things get in life, we still must be thankful for everything we have. Put things into perspective and enjoy the good things in your life.

46. You Don't Always Have To Be Happy

Being in a down mood is OK sometimes. You don't always have to be upbeat, excited, and outgoing. This could lead to burnout or a blowup. There are days when things aren't going right or we just feel a little out of it. These days are OK, and the problems will pass.

47. Think About It

Look at problems logically. When you let emotions take over, you may do things that made sense at the time but in the end weren't the best choices.

48. Don't Join the Gossip

Don't join in on the negative conversations around you. If you see a conversation heading down that road, excuse yourself politely and leave.

49. Start in the Right Direction

Wake up with a smile and with energy. You have a lot to accomplish and enjoy today. Life is short, and you are going to make the most of this day and of every day after it.

50. Never Stop Learning

This is the most important lesson of all. Never stop learning about the world around you. Read, listen, and learn about the things that interest you. Instead of asking a question and being satisfied with an "I don't know" answer, go and find the answer. Be curious. Attitude is everything. These tips will help you create a winning attitude and help others to do the same.

MOTIVATION MYTHS

Many people have goals in mind but don't take the steps to achieve them. Why? Because of the myths they believe in. Following are some of the major myths that people believe, and why you should avoid them.

I can't do it.
Yes, you can! What others have done, you can do. With the same size brain, same two arms and legs, and with the same amount of time during each day, men and women have done extraordinary things. What they did, you can also do.

I can start tomorrow.
Maybe you can't. Never put off things that you can do today. Tomorrow is never a guarantee, and no one can know what the future holds. All you can be sure of is that right now, this moment, you are here and can accomplish your goals.

It may not be right for me.
You'll never be 100 percent sure that what you are striving for is the perfect thing for you. This process takes time, and you will make many turns along the way. Don't wait for the perfect opportunity to knock on your door. You must go after it yourself.

START TODAY

Whatever goal you may have, whatever dream you want to achieve, start today. You can go about your days and weeks like you have been doing for the past few years, or you can set a goal, dedicate yourself to it, and do what it takes to make it come true.

I'll start tomorrow.
I'll start this summer.
I'll start when I graduate.
I'll start when the kids get out of school.
I'll start when the kids go back to school.
I'll start when the weather gets better.
I'll start when I get a new job.
I'll start when the moment is right.

The moment *is* right. Start today.

Appendix H

COMMITMENT

By A. Russell Chandler, III
Founder and former owner, Qualicare

In 1983, and for several years after I sold the healthcare company that I had founded 12 years before, I spoke often to college undergraduates and MBAs, listing the 10-12 key elements of success. After all, I, as graduate of Georgia Tech and the Wharton School of Business, possessed significant training and knowledge. Success certainly had to be a complex combination of applying all of that great knowledge with a tremendous work ethic and insight. When I sold the plastics company 10 years later and, being perhaps a bit more insightful, I streamlined this list to five or six key elements of success. Some items on the first list just didn't' seem appropriate anymore, particularly as I was able to analyze not only my own experiences but also those of other entrepreneurs whom I had had the opportunity of observing.

A few years later, after my once-in-a-lifetime Olympic experience, I concluded that success is really determined by two things: one controllable, the other not. As for the former, it was simply one word: commitment. I am convinced that one's degree of success is directly related to one's commitment to succeed. The term "driven" so often is used to describe successful athletes, coaches, businessmen, politicians, even ministers. But is that term ever used to describe unsuccessful people? Certainly not. And the truly committed person sets aside personal impediments to achieving the goals he or she has established. Simply stated, that is what it takes to emerge at the zenith of the competitive world.

Unfortunately, this commitment can have a down side. That is why the connotation of a "driven" person is often negative. Driven people can become so committed to a single objective that other aspects of a fruitful life (such as family, friends, health, integrity, morals, etc.) may become compromised. In the development of my company Qualicare, I would estimate that my typical workweek exceeded 100 hours and that I was on the road, on average, four days a week. I had no vacation for nine years. As distasteful as that sounds to me today, it was wonderful and exciting – not for the financial reward but for the satisfaction of creating and growing a successful and worthwhile enterprise. That essential commitment was possible then only because there was no family to be compromised at that time. With a wife and three daughters today, I could not, and would not, make such compromises. And today, balance is more important to me than any success in business.

Interestingly, however, the most important aspect of our success is uncontrolled by us; rather, it is the gift and plan that God has given us. Yet we often overlook this and claim all victories as if they were totally our own. Lest we forget, the single most important variable in determining our destiny is one thing we have no control over: our conception. We have not one single vote in determining our gene pool, circumstances, or the environment in which we are raised in our critical foundational years. How could I possibly argue that my life would have been no different if I had been raised in Memphis, Egypt, rather than Memphis, Tennessee? Or if I had been born to a family with little work ethic or upward mobility, or had been severely disabled? I couldn't. And my point is only this: all our skills, intelligence, motivation, personality traits, and opportunities are gifts from God. Thus, we must be mindful not to take too much of the credit for our own successes. The Bible reminds us that we will be judged not by the absolute amount of accomplishments we have on earth, but by what we do with that which has been given to us. Of those to whom much has been given, much will be required, so we had better recognize that and, as we are blessed, be prepared to share those blessings.

Not coincidentally, these same concepts apply to the principles essential to successful leadership. Commitment is observable and infectious; it inspires those around us. Once others realize their leader is committed not only to the success of the endeavor but also to them, they too must rise to the occasion — or else they will fall by the wayside. Likewise, as we each humble ourselves in admitting to the influence and value of God throughout their lives, they too can find their own blessings and exceed their own prior expectations. As a result, inspired coworkers create great leaders and sustain successful endeavors.

Appendix I

INFLUENCES ON THE MANUSCRIPT FOR LEADERSHIP FITNESS

The following people contributed not only inspiration to *Leadership Fitness* but also generously offered to write text to be incorporated into the manuscript for this book. They made this book complete.

Dr. Alexander Bralley, Founder, Metametrix Clinical Laboratory

Dr. John Cantwell, Chief Medical Officer 1996 Olympic Games

Russ Chandler, Founder, Qualicare and United Plastic Film

Dr. G. Wayne Clough, President, Georgia Institute of Technology

Bill Curry, ESPN Football Analyst

Randall W. Engle, Chair, School of Psychology, College of Sciences, Georgia Tech

Dan Freeman, Ranch Foreman, Augusta, MT

Don Harp, Senior Minister, Peachtree Road United Methodist Church

Hubert Harris, Chairman, Invesco Retirement, Inc.

Dr. Bevel Jones, Bishop, United Methodist Church

Jack Kinder, President, Kinder & Associates, Dallas, TX

Martha Lanier, President, "Igniting Unlimited Potential"

Jim Lientz, President, Mid-South Bank of America, and Chief
    Operating Officer for Georgia Governor Sonny Perdue

Carolyn Luesing, President, Luesing & Associates

Jack Markwalter, Head of Atlanta Trust Co., NA

Hank McCamish, Chairman of the Board, McCamish Group

Bill Moore, Founder, Chairman of the Board, Kelly-Moore Paint Co.

John D. Morgan, Executive Director, Omicron Delta Kappa Society, Inc.

Andrés Núñez, Co-founder, TEI Engineers and Planners

Albert Bud Parker, Beck & Gregg Hardware Co.

Dr. Chris Rosenbloom, Associate Professor, Georgia State University

Bud Shaw, Founder, Chairman of the Board, Shaw Industries

Dal Shealy, President, Fellowship of Christian Athletes

Eddie Smith, Grady White Boat Co., Founder and Chairman of the Board

Carl Stevens, President, Carl Stevens & Associates, Inc.

John Williams, Founder, Post Properties, Inc.

Rick Worsham, Founder, Worsham & Sammons, Inc.

It has been a pleasure each year to invite Dave Braine, the highly successful Director of Athletics at Georgia Tech, and members of his staff to address my class. A number of people from his office gave presentations to the 2003 Leadership Fitness class.

Rob Skinner, Director, Homer Rice Center for Sports Performance and
    the Student-Athlete Total Person Program

Mary McElroy, Senior Associate Athletic Director

Allison George, Director of Communications

Kyleen Bell, Staff and former outstanding student-athlete

Larry New, Senior Associate Athletic Director

Over the years, many people have given of their time to share their experience and knowledge with my Georgia Tech classes. The final manuscript owes a debt to their past efforts.

Arthur Blank, Founder, Home Depot

Charles Brady, Executive Chairman, Invesco

Don Chapman, CEO, Tug Manufacturing Corp.

Mark Dash, Partner, Goldman Sachs & Co.

A.D. Frazier, CEO, Invesco

John Imlay, President, Imlay Investments

Dr. Randy Martin, Dean, Emory University Clinical Development

Shirley C. Newborn, V.P., Southern Engineering Co.

Dr. William Osher, Director of Success Programs, Georgia Tech

Pete Petite, Chairman, Healthdyne, Inc.

Dr. Catherine Ross, Former Executive Director, GRTA
    Currently Director of the Center for Quality Growth and Regional
    Development, Georgia Tech

Dr. Gary Schuster, Dean, Georgia Tech College of Science

W. Thomas Smith, V.P., IBM

John Wallace, Senior Partner, King & Spalding

Ambassador Andrew Young, Chairman, Good Works International

INDEX